**handbooks**

# Overseas Job Hunting

## on the internet

Using the internet to find great opportunities
anywhere in the world

Laurel Alexander
MCIPD MICG

www.internet-handbooks.co.uk

*Other Internet Handbooks by the same author*

Careers Guidance on the Internet
Education & Training on the Internet
Graduate Job Hunting on the Internet
Human Resource Management on the Internet
Working from Home on the Internet

First published in 2001 by Internet Handbooks Ltd, Plymbridge House,
Estover Road, Plymouth PL6 7PY, United Kingdom.

Customer services tel:          (01752) 202301
Orders fax:                     (01752) 202333
Customer services email:        cservs@plymbridge.com
Distributors web site:          www.plymbridge.com
Internet Handbooks web site:    www.internet-handbooks.co.uk

Laurel Alexander has asserted her moral right to be identified as the author of
this work.

Note: The contents of this book are offered for the purposes of general
guidance only and no liability can be accepted for any loss or expense incurred
as a result of relying in particular circumstances on statements made in this
book. Readers are advised to check the current position with the appropriate
authorities before entering into personal arrangements.

Typeset by PDQ Typesetting, Newcastle Under Lyme
Printed and bound by The Cromwell Press Ltd, Trowbridge, Wiltshire.

# Contents

# Contents......................................................

# List of illustrations

7

# Preface

With the rise and rise of the internet, the world is truly becoming a global village. In the old days, if you wanted to work abroad, it could take months of letter writing and phone calls to unearth the necessary information. By the time you had done your research you might easily have missed out on the best opportunities. Today, the internet has transformed the whole process, opening up amazing new possibilities for working abroad. From the comfort of your computer keyboard you can explore current job vacancies in countries all over the world; you can quickly find out about local living conditions, read the local press, make contact with local expats, identify specialist recruitment agencies, post your CV into online databases, email prospective employers, and apply to firms direct online. This book aims to provide a practical springboard for your new working life abroad, together with hundreds of key web links to get you started.

There are of course pitfalls for the would-be expatriate worker. Among these are language barriers, cultural shocks and social problems, unexpected costs, problems with the right qualifications, and health hazards. Again the internet comes into its own. You can use the power of the world wide web and other aspects of the internet to surmount these barriers. For example you can learn a language online, explore the local culture, check out the local living conditions, acquire some extra skills and knowledge, and ensure that your qualifications are acceptable in your host country.

Working overseas is undoubtedly exciting, and it can add an extremely valuable dimension to your career profile for the future. You will learn how to work with people of different cultures and how to tackle some challenging problems in an unfamiliar environment. If you want to be an international worker, but without physically relocating, the internet can even enable you to provide a home-based service to clients on the other side of the world.

As a professional assessor and guidance specialist, I have had the privilege of helping many people make successful transitions in their working lives. I hope that, among all the information contained in this book, you will find everything you need to succeed in the overseas jobs market. Good luck!

*Laurel Alexander*
*laurelalexander@internet-handbooks.co.uk*

# 1 The internet for jobseekers

**In this chapter we will explore:**

▶ *about the internet*
▶ *the internet and the jobseeker*
▶ *some things you can do on the internet*
▶ *accessing the internet*
▶ *using the internet as a jobseeker*
▶ *problems with accessing web addresses*
▶ *electronic recruitment and placement*

## About the internet

The internet is the largest network of computers that the world has ever seen. Today, it spans more than 110 countries and reaches over 270 million people. The word 'internet' is given to a collection of computers around the world that can be connected to each other using ordinary telephone lines.

The internet began in America in the 1960s. It all started with a network of four computers owned by the Department of Defense, known as ARPANET. The idea was to swap information between agency sites in the event of a nuclear attack which might destroy one or other of the computers. The early internet was used exclusively by engineers, scientists and computer experts, long before the days of home or office personal computers.

Fig. 1. Arpanet, the beginnings of the US-based computer network that has evolved into today's global internet.

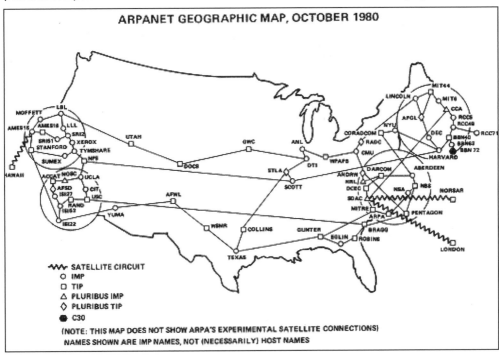

ARPANET GEOGRAPHIC MAP, OCTOBER 1980

SATELLITE CIRCUIT
○ IMP
□ TIP
△ PLURIBUS IMP
◇ PLURIBUS TIP
● C30

[NOTE: THIS MAP DOES NOT SHOW ARPA'S EXPERIMENTAL SATELLITE CONNECTIONS]
NAMES SHOWN ARE IMP NAMES, NOT (NECESSARILY) HOST NAMES

# The internet for jobseekers ...............................................

**Internet Explorer**

**Netscape Navigator**

Fig. 2. Browser toolbars. You must have a browser to explore the internet. The two great rivals (both free) are Microsoft's Internet Explorer and Netscape Navigator. Internet Explorer is slightly easier to use, and integrates better with other Microsoft programs.

Another milestone in the emergence of the internet was passed at the European Laboratory for Particle Physics in Switzerland in 1989. From there developed the concept of a world wide network – or 'web' – of computers. It was based on the technique of hypertext links which enable any computer linked to the web to access information stored on any other computer linked to the web.

Around this time web browsers were also created. Marc Andreessen at the National Centre for Supercomputing Applications became the brains behind Netscape Corporation which produced the first really successful graphical type of web browser (Netscape Navigator). Soon, Microsoft developed its own very similar competing browser, Internet Explorer, which has since overtaken Netscape in popularity. 1990 saw the first commercial company to provide access to the internet. The 1990s saw the information superhighway (a term first used by American Vice President Al Gore) really taking off.

▶ *Internet* – A general term which encompasses the technologies of electronic mail (email), web pages, internet chat, newsgroups, internet mailing lists, bulletin board services, video conferencing, telnet, and various others. What they all have in common is that they are based on people using computers linked together in a global network using telephone and satellite communications.

Focusing on the UK, a survey conducted by MORI research found that:

1.  Over ten million people are online.
2.  One in ten UK users now describe themselves as regularly online.
3.  40 per cent of British users have gone online in the past twelve months.
4.  Users spend five hours or less online per week, visiting 13 web sites in that time.
5.  Women account for 43 per cent of British users
6.  9 per cent of the over 55s are online

It is difficult to know exactly how many people are online throughout the world. However, Nua Internet Surveys indicated in February 2000 that the figure was around 275.5 million. It must be a good deal higher now.

## The internet and the jobseeker

As an international job searcher, you will want to know how the internet can work for you. Above all, the internet is an incredible source of free information. From the comfort of your PC, you can easily access millions of web sites across the globe, web sites which provide information on such topics as occupations, career management, vocational training, contract work, permanent and temporary work, and worldwide free-lance opportunities. The internet can link you into sites offering all kinds of work in any country. There are country-specific sites providing a wealth of background information on living and working conditions. And you can link to these opportunities in seconds, at the click of your mouse. The internet is by far the most powerful resource available to international jobseekers today.

## Some things you can do on the internet

| | |
|---|---|
| apply for a job | organise a virtual therapy session |
| arrange a career development session | play music |
| book flights, hotels and car hire | post Easter greetings across the world |
| buy any product or service | promote a business |
| check your bank balance | read and post messages in newsgroups |
| compare prices | read bulletin boards |
| consult a financial advisor | read overseas newspapers |
| contact recruitment consultants | receive electronic newsletters |
| despatch faxes from your computer | research into companies |
| develop new business contacts | save money by finding bargains |
| distribute your CV | search for long-lost relatives |
| download a book | search through jobs databases |
| download free programs | see what NASA are up to |
| earn money | seek out a romantic partner |
| enjoy free stuff of all kinds | sell anything |
| find out everything about anything | send and receive email |
| fix up a holiday | send and receive text and other files |
| follow a football club | shop online |
| get an astrological reading | study for a qualification |
| join a videoconference | test your skills |
| link into a satellite from space | track down job opportunities world- |
| log into a chatroom | wide |
| look up a medical condition | tune in to live internet radio programmes |
| make telephone calls | view the latest sports results |
| obtain legal advice | write to the President of the USA |
| order specialist food and drink | |

## Accessing the internet

In order to get onto the internet you need the following:

▶ *Computer* – The minimum hardware you would need would be an IBM-compatible 486 computer or a Macintosh 6803 series with an absolute minimum of 8 megabytes of RAM (temporary memory). A modern computer priced around £1,000 would typically have 32 to 128 megabytes of temporary memory, a hard drive of anywhere from

5 to 20 gigabytes, and a speed of anywhere from 200 to 700 mega-hertz. The computer will normally come with a monitor, keyboard, mouse, and preferably a pair of speakers, all of which plug into the back of the computer box.

▶ *Modem* – You could have an internal modem which slots into the main processing board of your computer, out of sight. A desktop (external) modem sits alongside your computer and plugs into the back. Both plug into any ordinary phone socket. Finally there are hand-held modems which can be used with portable computers.

Fig. 3. Internet service providers. Most ISPs supply customers with an easy-to-use installation CD rom. Pop it into your computer, and it will install everything you need to connect to and use the internet. Illustrated are Freeserve, Virgin Net, Madasafish, and America OnLine.

▶ *Printer* – Get yourself either a colour inkjet printer, or a black and white laser printer. Laser printers give excellent pin-sharp quality for letters and CVs. Colour laser printers, however, are still extremely expensive.

▶ *Internet access provider (IAP) or internet service provider (ISP)* – The former type of company enables a user to connect to the internet via a modem connected to the user's computer. An internet service provider offers a range of its own services (shopping, music, news, chat, email, newsgroups etc) in addition to the all-important general internet access. Examples of well-known ISPs in the UK include America

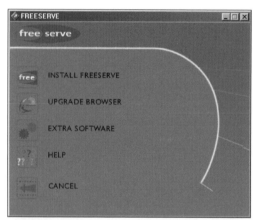

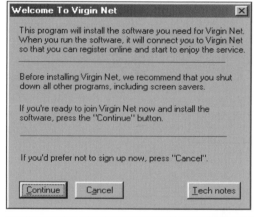

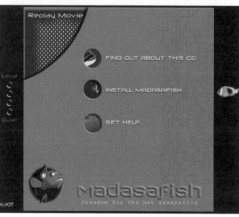

Online, BT Internet, Compuserve, Demon, FreeUK, Freeserve, Madasafish, and Virgin Net.

If you don't have direct access to the internet, you could try one of the many high-street cyber cafés, the local library, your local careers office, or twist the arm of a willing friend.

## Using the internet as a jobseeker

The internet can be used:

1   As a portal to a vast amount of occupational and employer information.

2.   For access to online careers guidance services.

3.   For professional networking, such as by email.

4.   For electronic recruitment and placement.

5.   To find freelance work.

### Information portals

A portal is a web site that serves as a gateway or jumping-off point to the internet, or to some particular part of it. It consists of an edited web page or pages of links and services designed to guide users quickly to the relevant information. Examples:

▶  Yahoo! – one of the best general internet portal sites (http://www.yahoo.com).

▶  Escape Artist – a big portal site specially developed for expatriates (http://www.escapeartist.com).

Fig. 4. Escape Artist is an essential bookmark for overseas jobhunters.

# The internet for jobseekers ·····································

*Computer-assisted guidance*
This technology refers to facilities such as file transfer, database access and downloadable material; for example:

▶ JobBank USA – which offers a resume database service (see page 111).

*Networking through bulletin boards*
You can use the internet to network with fellow professionals, which in turn may lead to work offers. This can be achieved via reading and posting messages on bulletin board services (BBS). A BBS is a computer system with network access which serves as an information and message-passing centre for remote users. Users dial into a BBS with their modems and post messages to other BBS users. It is rather like posting messages on a corkboard. Some BBSs allow users to chat online and download and upload files.

*Networking through newsgroups*
A newsgroup is a kind of public electronic bulletin board on the internet where individuals from anywhere in the world can post (like sending email) all kinds of messages.

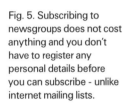

Fig. 5. Subscribing to newsgroups does not cost anything and you don't have to register any personal details before you can subscribe - unlike internet mailing lists.

▶ *Newsgroup* – Usenet discussion groups. Each newsgroup is a collection of messages, usually unedited and not checked by anyone ('unmoderated'). Messages can be read and posted in the newsgroup by anyone, including you. The 80,000-plus newsgroups in existence are collectively referred to as Usenet.

Anyone can subscribe to a newsgroup, and unsubscribe, instantaneously and as often as you like. To access newsgroups, you need a

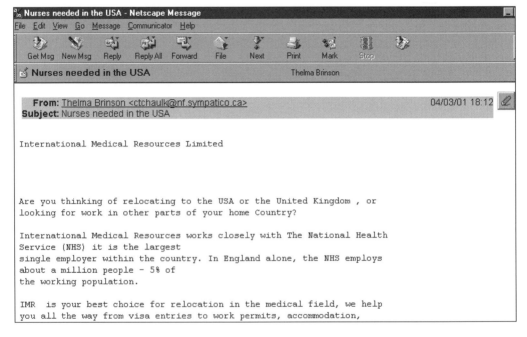

newsgroup supplier, called a 'news server' (usually provided by your ISP), and news reading software. The latter is usually Outlook Express (for Internet Explorer users) and Messenger (for Netscape users). The following newsgroups might be worth a visit:

| Name of newsgroup | Description |
|---|---|
| alt.jobs.overseas | a big general jobs newsgroup |
| aus.ads.jobs | for jobs in Australia |
| us.jobs.offered | for jobs in the USA |

*Internet mailing lists*

This term refers to online forums in which people communicate about subjects of common interest. To access a mailing list, you first need to find one of interest, and then subscribe to it. The best place on the internet to find mailing lists is Liszt which links to more than 90,000 different lists, arranged in helpful categories:

http://www.liszt.com

Fig. 6. Liszt directory contains links to more than 90,000 different mailing lists. Liszt is an excellent source if you want to find an email list that covers your favourite topic. Just search for your interest and follow the instructions for subscribing to the list.

*Marketing tool for advertising your skills*

The internet is a superb medium for round-the-clock, year-round global advertising. You could even create and publish your own web page and advertise your services.

*Finding out more*

▶ *Discussion Forums on the Internet*, by Kye Valongo (Internet Handbooks), a practical step-by-step illustrated guide to newsgroups, mailing lists and bulletin board services.

▶ *Creating a Home Page on the Internet*, by Richard Cochrane, a practical step-by-step guide for everyone.

## Problems with accessing web addresses

It can sometimes be a problem accessing a particular world wide web page. In case this happens to you, here are some tips to help you.

1. First, make certain you have entered the URL correctly, since there is no room for error in the spelling either of words or of special characters.

2. Next, try to access the site again later. Even the best known sites are sometimes overwhelmed by traffic or temporarily closed for maintenance.

3. If that doesn't work, strip the URL back to its root address (in case the site's individual web pages have been reorganised) and try again. For example:

> http://www.sitename.com/folder/page.html
> http://www.sitename.com

4. Finally, the site may have moved to a new URL, without leaving a forwarding link. If so, try using one of the search engines mentioned in chapter 5 of this book. If that fails too, the site may for some reason have been withdrawn from service. In this case the search engine may suggest some useful alternatives.

## Electronic recruitment and placement

There is a massive boom in online recruitment agencies. They may require CVs to be submitted online and they may offer an email service to keep you informed about suitable vacancies. There are also web sites that offer electronic posting of vacancies but don't match client with vacancy – which is down to the individual.

There are many internet resources for creating online CVs. One of the best is Jobsearch. This allows you to create CVs that can be accessed by UK employers using the JobSearch database:

> http://www.jobsearch.co.uk

Another site worth visiting is Monsterboard:

> http://www.monsterboard.com

This is a good source of vacancies. You can also access its CV Builder page to complete a pro-forma CV or to submit your own. Note: some organisations charge a fee for their CV-building services.

### More Internet Handbooks to help you
*Finding a Job on the Internet*, Brendan Murphy. 2nd edition.
*Graduate Job Hunting on the Internet*, Laurel Alexander.
*Where to Find It on the Internet*, Kye Valongo. 2nd edition.

# 2 The global jobs market

**In this chapter we will explore:**

► *teleworking*
► *worldwide freelancing*
► *finding temporary work worldwide*
► *the worldwide contract worker*
► *holiday jobs and exchanges*
► *voluntary work abroad*

. . . . . . . . . . . . . . . . . . . . . . . . . . . . . . . . . . . . . . . . . . . . . . . . . . . . . . . . . . . . . . . . . . . .

The global job market today offers a variety of career paths for the international jobhunter. You could be an international teleworker working from home using technology, either for an employer or for yourself. You can use the internet for global freelancing. You could set up as a freelance teleworker, based almost anywhere in the world, or you could run an ecommerce service of some kind, again from almost any location in the world where you can arrange internet access.

Overseas temporary work is another alternative. It offers the chance to have a year out, take a sabbatical in another country, or 'try before you buy' into a more permanent overseas way of life.

## Teleworking

*Getting started*
Teleworking involves some start-up costs, notably the computer as well as a modem and a printer. A rewritable CD-ROM is also a good idea as you can then save a large volume of work on one disk ready to be sent back to an employer or client. A scanner will widen the scope of work

Fig. 7. The Teleworking Jobs web site is a useful starting point for information.

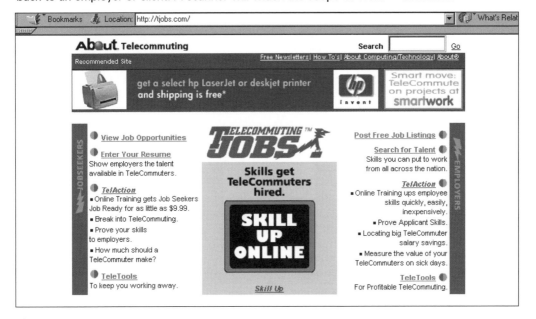

17

you can take on involving the processing of pictures and documents. Scanners can also be used for inputting a text document into a word processing package for changes to be made.

Minor costs involve supplies of floppy disks, printing paper, plus inks or toner cartridges for printers. An allowance should be made for extra electricity used and slightly higher telephone bills as most of your communications will be made via the telephone. Of course if you work for an employer, they will provide all this equipment – if you work for yourself, the buck stops with you.

### The trend

Attracted by a flexible working lifestyle and lucrative project rates, an increasing number of people with new media skills are choosing to set up their own small internet businesses. For clients looking to buy new media services, outsourcing to small businesses or freelancers means they can avoid the fixed costs associated with maintaining employees in-house, or paying the high fees charged by full-service agencies. According to the TCA (Telework, Telecottage and Telecentre Association), more than 1.3 million people in the UK now telework using electronic communications, without attending a formal workplace.

### A survey

Based on the UK Labour Force Survey of Spring 1997, the Teleworker Magazine reports that the current number of teleworkers in Great Britain is 987,000, which is 4 per cent of total employment. One third of employed teleworkers are in banking, finance and insurance.

### European Telework Online
http://www.eto.org.uk
This is a useful internet portal for teleworking, telecommuting, and related topics. It links into more than 2,500 places on the internet worldwide.

Work at Home Workforce
**TELECOMMUTING JOBS**

How to search TeleCommuting jobs without killing TeleCommuting.

### Telecommuting Jobs
http://tjobs.com
From the home page of this site you can explore telecommuting with employers in the US or anywhere else in the world. There are opportunities for artists, writers, web designers, data entry staff, desktop publishers, engineers, programmers, sales people and photographers. There are links to an online newsletter and other resources. You can view around 60,000 telecommuting work-from-home job opportunities, and enter your résumé.

### Telelink Training for Europe
http://www.marble.ac.uk/telep/telework/tlpfolder/tlp.html
The Telelink Training for Europe project is a European Community, Euroform-funded project which seeks to develop training opportunities in the field of teleworking. The Telework for Europe project aims to establish transnational, vocational qualifications and training for telework skills. This project has already defined a level II, Restricted Vocational

Qualification (RVQ) for teleworkers. The TeleLink Training for Europe project has established a growing network of TeleLink Centres (telecottages and training centres) around Europe that can provide training support and service points for telework skills. The TeleLink project has also developed a level III, National Vocational Qualification (NVQ) for teleworker supervisors and is currently defining a third, level IV, Vocational Qualification for telecottage managers.

*Telework Training Resources*
http://www.icbl.hw.ac.uk/telep/telework/ttrfolder/typfolder/typ.html
The directory section is designed to provide teleworkers with a directory for information on various telework organisations, associations, projects and services. It covers the UK and Europe.

## Worldwide freelancing

On the internet, distance has virtually no meaning. You can collaborate, submit your work, do research and work from almost anywhere in the world. The global marketplace is going to become not only a market for products, but also a market for services and talent. Although freelancing has been around for ages, the internet makes it particularly easy to work remotely, especially on computer software, web development, writing, reporting, and sales. In addition, the internet makes it very easy to find jobs, regardless of where you live.

There are many web sites with job listings for contractors. In addition, many job-listing sites also offer contract positions. The latest twist in freelancing is the auctioning of talent. The first type of auction is one where freelance contractors (mainly software and web developers) post their availability and skills for employers to bid on (Monster.com Talent Market). This is beneficial to workers, because it allows them to maximise their wages. However the problem is that most companies are not interested in getting into a bidding war over freelance workers with whom they have no prior experience. EXP.com focuses on selling knowledge and expert advice. Experts post their qualifications and rates. People can then pick an expert, based on price or qualifications, and ask a question.

Turning things around, the other way to get freelance jobs is to bid on projects. Elance.com is one company using this model. This is a very promising idea because companies have a great incentive to use companies like eLance. By posting a project, they solicit bids on the internet. Then they can pick the best qualified or the most inexpensive contractor for the project. The global reach of the internet allows people from all over the world to bid on projects.

As a freelancer you are self-employed and are responsible for marketing your business, delivering your business, financial management and business planning. You could choose to be a portfolio freelance and have several areas of expertise to offer. The more you can offer, the more money you can make and the less likely you are to be out of work.

*Ideas for general freelancing*

| | |
|---|---|
| Authoring web pages | Legal services |
| Brokering services | Online auctions |
| Customised products | Recruitment agency |
| Data conversion | Research |
| Dating agency | Selling collectibles |
| DTP | Selling emailing lists |
| Setting up databases | Selling of shippable goods |
| Ebook writing and publishing | Shareware |
| Ecommerce consultancy | Tourism services |
| Financial services | Translation |
| Graphic design | Writing articles and reports |
| Information brokering | Writing/selling software |

*Ants.com*

http://www.ants.com/ants/

This site offers to match freelancers with businesses who want to out-source projects that can be completed remotely.

*Consult Direct*

http://www.kelwin.co.uk/ConsultDirect/bout.htm

Here you can find an unaffiliated directory of consultants, freelancers and contractors. Advertisers can present themselves with a company profile, a CV or a résumé.

*Freelance.com*

http://www.freelance.com

Freelance.com is a new online professional services marketplace that connects pre-screened freelance professionals around the world with Fortune 1000 and market-leading companies that need them every day. It says it is the only global online professional services network offering companies a dedicated Account Manager to ensure excellent matches and long-term support. It aims to meet the exploding needs of multinational and regional companies nearly anywhere. Originally established

Fig. 8. Freelance.com has developed an impressive service for global networkers.

in France in 1996, Freelance.com is now headquartered in New York, and has offices in 14 countries worldwide.

*Freelance BBS*
http://www.freelancebbs.com
The Freelance Bulletin Board Service helps freelancers and their prospective employers to find each other. Using a simple online form, you can either search for a project or a talented individual in several professions. They say: 'Feel free to post projects and availabilities. For more precise results, you can try using two advanced search forms: one for available projects and another one for freelancers in search of work.' After you post your ad (whether it's a résumé or a job availability), you can still make changes to it or delete it if necessary. To do that, find your ad through the search form, go to 'details' and look for the Modify and Delete buttons at the bottom of the ad. You will be asked for the password which you chose when posting your ad.

*Freelance Informer*
http://www.freelanceinformer.co.uk
Resources for the IT contracting sector can be found through this home page. You can register to access job postings, news, information on recruiters and training, and advice for new contractors. There are links to directory, finance, first timers, IR35, jobs, legal, news, overseas, skills and a yearbook. 'There are 3,299 jobs today at Freelance Informer.' The service is a division of Reed Business Information.

*Freelance Jobs*
http://www.freelance-jobs.net
Freelance Jobs describes itself as a major source of jobs, career advancement opportunities, and employment information for the freelance industry.

*Freelance Marketplace*
http://247malls.com/OS/cj/ants.htm
This is where you can find your marketplace community for independent contractors and freelance opportunities. They say: 'Welcome to your freelance marketplace, your marketplace community for independent contractors and businesses Browse through the job listing to find freelance opportunities that match your interests including writing, marketing, translation, programming and design.'

*Freelance Online*
http://www.freelanceonline.com
The operators of the site say that they intend to make it a primary resource centre for small business owners and the self-employed. You can access jobs, message boards, a searchable directory of over 700 freelancers, frequently asked questions, resources, and networking opportunities for freelance professionals. Run from Philadelphia, USA, the site serves freelancers and employers already established in the web community and those who are new to the web. The fee for full mem-

bership is $15 per year. This includes a listing in the directory and access to the jobs page. Freelancers can post their profiles with FOL and can even obtain links to their own home pages (a reciprocal link is appreciated but not mandatory). 'Browse through our directory and find the group or groups that best fit your skills, then register your information with us.' In the Open Forum you can discuss issues with other freelancers. The resource area lists helpful links and information on various aspects of freelancing. The service was launched in 1996.

### Freelancers.net
http://www.freelancers.net
Freelancers.net maintains an open database of UK and global internet freelancers. It costs nothing to get yourself listed and it is free to search for freelancers: 'Matching freelance and contract internet and multimedia professionals to freelance and contract opportunities.' The Freelancers Network gives you your own easy-to-remember web address which you can point to your own portfolio, CV, or résumé.

### Freelance Work Exchange
http://www.freelanceworkexchange.com
The site offers a free report describing 50 top-producing freelance markets, together with a freelance directory and project directory.

### FreetimeJobs.com
http://www.freejob.com
This site seeks to match ordinary people of all skill levels with small businesses that need help. From a few hours of seasonal work to longer term projects, there are lots of opportunities to explore.

### Guru
http://www.guru.com
Founded in 1999, Guru.com describes itself as the web's premier

Fig. 9. The home page of Guru.com.

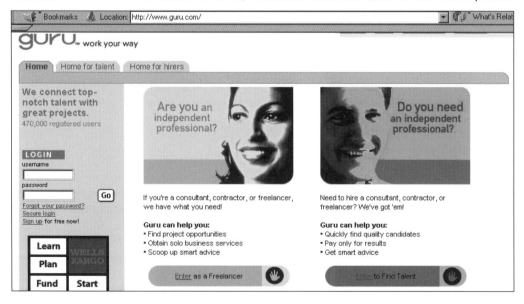

exchange for connecting independent professionals with contract projects. With more than 300,000 independent professionals and over 30,000 hiring clients registered by late 2000, Guru has been recognized as a top-ranking resource by *PC Magazine*, Yahoo!, *Internet Life*, *Forbes* and other industry leaders. Based in San Francisco, it has raised $63 million from investors to develop its services. They say: 'Our convenient online system makes it easy to log billable hours, manage your expenses, and generate invoices Our street-smart articles and advice columns help you tackle the challenges of guru life.' Registration is free.

*HireAbility*
http://www.hireability.com
This is a service company that provides a link between businesses needing specialised work performed and those with the ability to get the job done. It offers freelancing, telecommuting, contract, consulting, writing, artistic, marketing, sales and other types of work.

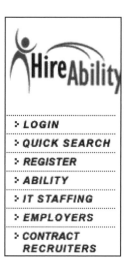

*Hit Squad Freelancers*
http://www.hitsquad.co.uk/free.htm
This sites the freelancer DTP professionals or 'Hitsquadders'. So if you are PC or MAC ready, a visit to this site might bring in some work. Click on freelance or vacancy to access opportunities.

*Jobsunlimited*
http://www.jobsunlimited.co.uk
You can search for freelance work in the *The Guardian* and *Observer* newspapers here.

*Outsource 2000*
http://outsource2000.com
Outsource2000 has joined forces with leading sources in the home-based work related industry to create an online forum where individuals throughout the north America and the rest of the world can now get continuously updated information relating to áll aspects' of working from home. They say: 'Inside our Home Workers Forum is an unparalleled selection of home-based jobs and opportunities, over 50 separate job search databases, and everything else needed to make your future as a home-based worker complete.' The company has been developing home-based work related programs, products, and services since 1993.

*Smarterwork*
http://www.smarterwork.com
You can get the job done – 100 per cent online. Smarterwork describes itself as the complete virtual office. You will find the right people, a secure environment, and all the tools you need to work with others on projects. And the global payment system ensures that you really can do business with people all over the world. Freelance work includes writing, editing, graphic design, web build support, and document production. The site includes special sections on start-ups and small/medium businesses.

# The global jobs market......................................................

*The Business*
http://www.thebusinessuk.com
This site promotes business in the UK and throughout the world. You can link into loans, advice, opportunities, and information. The site provides free links, free offers, and interesting contacts and fraud watch pages as well as provocative news and press releases.

*Vault*
http://www.vault.com
Vault is an email-based job search and job matching service. It also sells industry guides, employer profiles and insider research, and runs various message boards. As well as offering a wealth of free jobs information and career advice, it also has a whole channel devoted to freelancing, and hosts a busy freelance marketplace.

## Finding temporary work worldwide

Areas of international temporary employment include:

1. adventure travel companies
2. camping firms
3. ski resort companies
4. Teaching English as a Foreign Language (TEFL)
5. voluntary organisations
6. work camps (run by voluntary organisations)

## The worldwide contract worker

Some of the main industries which employ Europe-wide contract workers include:

| | |
|---|---|
| IT | aerospace |
| electronics | defence |
| railway | nuclear |
| public utilities | agriculture |
| telecommunications | medical |
| ship building | construction |
| mining | power generation |

Beyond Europe there are opportunities in, for example, North America, Taiwan, Indonesia and the new democracies of Eastern Europe. If you want to become a worldwide contractor, you need to:

1. Prepare a portfolio of CVs.

2. Establish your contract book (containing agents' contact points).

Most contracts are operated on a limited company basis. If you find work through an agent, most of them will insist on your setting up as a limited company. Talk to your accountant to find out whether and how you should become incorporated. Establish what your liabilities are likely to be for corporation tax, national insurance, dividend income, and income tax, and what expenses you can offset against tax.

There are three different components of the contracting profession. The first is the contractor (you). The second is the agency that recruits and hires contractors. The third component is the client company for whom the work is to be done.

*The client company*
The client company contracts with an agency to recruit and hire contractors to work on the client's project on a temporary job assignment. Let's assume that one of the thousands of client companies who often utilize contract personnel has a major project under way. They have tried to hire enough direct employees to staff that project but have been unsuccessful, and now find themselves falling behind schedule. The client can then turn to an agency and ask them to supply contract personnel in the job disciplines they require. Highly skilled contractors will then be employed by the agency to step in, normally side by side with the client's direct employees, to work on the project. As a contractor, working in this manner, you would be working on the client's project, under client supervision, but you would be an employee of the agency that placed you. They would give you your salary.

During the late 1990s another rationale has emerged for clients to hire contractors through staffing firms. Now we often see contract positions being advertised as 'contract to direct'. This is simply a 'try before you buy' approach. Both clients and contractors are more frequently checking each other out before committing to a long-term relationship.

*The method of working*
The commonest method is to work as an employee for an agency on assignment with that company's client. The agency normally finds the contract job opening, then employs you to work for their client. Or you can work through the same agency as an independent contractor instead of an employee. This method, however, involves more responsibility for the contractor and more risk to all three parties (contractor, agency and client). An independent contractor must pay his or her own taxes, insurance etc. A third way in which some people become contractors is to form their own company and work as employees of that corporation. Their company simply bills their clients for work performed. They then pay themselves out of corporate profits.

*A variety of contracting opportunities*
You will find contractors working in virtually every major industry in the world. These industries include software, aerospace, nuclear, computers, marine, petrochemical, manufacturing, electronic, entertainment, chemical, textile, financial, commercial, refinery, communications, publications, transportation, electrical, structural, mining etc. Typically, the length of a contract assignment is from six to nine months. Many last longer; some are shorter.

*The typical contractor*

Contractors are highly qualified, highly paid individuals. They have often obtained additional schooling and technical training in their field. They are therefore very well qualified to handle most jobs in their specific discipline. That is a major reason why they are usually paid more than their direct counterpart would be paid.

If this kind of work intrigues you, or you see it as an opportunity to find that dream job you have always been seeking, you'll need to prepare a professional résumé. Your résumé is generally the first contact you have with an agency and, often, the only contact with a client company until your first day on an assignment. So you must have an effective résumé. And, because most contract firms now scan, or in some manner, input all their résumés into a searchable database, your résumé needs to be presented in a manner that makes it easy to scan.

*Contract Employment Weekly*
http://www.ceweekly.wa.com
Through subscription, you can find jobs here in engineering, IT/IS and technical work.

*Contracts 365*
http://www.contracts365.com/search/
This site specialises in international contract work for IT professionals and lists job vacancies with submitted CVs going direct to the relevant agency.

## Holiday jobs and exchanges

*AIESEC*
http://www.uk.aiesec.org
AIESEC is the world's largest international, student-run organiser of international graduate exchanges and careers fairs. Represented in more than 80 countries, it has a membership of more than 50,000 people, including on 23 campuses in the UK. Its primary focus is on the exchange of graduates and undergraduates between various countries in the fields of business, management, finance, marketing, engineering and economics.

*American Work Experience*
http://www.awe-recruitment.freeserve.co.uk
AWE recruits European staff to work for about nine weeks in US children's summer camps. Applicants should be aged 18 to 31 and meet certain clearly stated criteria.

*British Universities North America Club*
http://www.bunac.org
BUNAC is a non-profit, non-political, student organisation with its own travel company. Formed in 1962 by students from North America Clubs and Canada Clubs at universities throughout the UK, BUNAC continues to be represented on British campuses by enthusiastic ex-participants. One of BUNACamp's founders, John Ball, began taking groups of camp counsellors to North America as long ago as 1953. Today, the organisa-

tion makes it possible for young people all over the world to participate in similar programmes worldwide.

*Central Bureau for Educational Visits & Exchanges*
http://www.britishcouncil.org/cbiet/
http://www.britcoun.org/cbeve/
This is an official UK body, established for many years, which promotes and organises annual programmes of visits and exchanges with schools and other educational organisations around the world.

*Council on International Educational Exchange*
http://www.ciee.org
Established for over 50 years, the CIEE provides a service to young people studying, working and travelling abroad.

*InternAbroad*
http://www.internabroad.com
InternAbroad is a comprehensive online source for international internships, study abroad, jobs abroad, volunteer positions abroad, teaching positions abroad and a whole lot more.

Fig. 10. Internet Abroad. Working on an internship programme is an excellent way of obtaining overseas work experience.

*Students Partnership Worldwide*
http://www.spw.org
This is a development charity that sends graduates on educational and environmental programmes in Africa and Asia for five months.

*SummerJobs*
http://www.summerjobs.com
This site offers a very brightly presented international listing of seasonal and summer employment opportunities. We searched the jobs database

for 'sports' jobs, and this yielded 20 vacancies (mostly in American summer camps). A search for 'driving' jobs produced 5 vacancies, and one for 'music' yielded 12. Employers can post jobs to the database for free. The site also contains a very useful collection of links to summer and temporary jobs, student jobs, and employment sources of various kinds.

China
Ghana
India
Mexico
Nepal
Peru
Romania
Russia
South Africa
Thailand
Togo
Ukraine

*Teaching Abroad*
http://www.teaching-abroad.co.uk
They say: 'Whether you teach with us in an Indian school or work with us on a conservation project in Mexico, whether you help with English classes in Moscow or do a veterinary project in Ghana, you will be in demand Programmes are eye-opening and life-changing, and also enjoyable and sensibly planned.'

*Vacation Work and Holiday Jobs*
http://www.elstead.co.uk/abroad.htm
This site offers a selection of guidebooks for students or anyone seeking temporary summer jobs abroad.

*Vacation Work Publications*
http://www.vacationwork.co.uk
Vacation Work is an Oxford-based publisher of a range of reference books and directories for jobs, travel and adventure.

*Working Holidays Abroad*
http://www.atlantica.co.uk/travel/newhaven.html
Have the adventure of a lifetime living and working in another country. A free report explains how you can have a working holiday anywhere in the world – Austria to the USA, the Bahamas to Israel, South Africa to Spain, fruit picking in Greece or working in ski resorts in North America. Kibbutzim, au pairs, and tourism are other possibilities.

*World Careers Network*
http://www.wcn.co.uk/main/
This is a large site with useful search facilities for UK university students looking for full-time, part-time, vacation, work experience and graduate placement schemes in the UK and Europe. Visitors can also search by regional vacancies.

## Voluntary work abroad

This section lists some of the best-known organisations in the field of overseas voluntary work.

*Ecovolunteer*
http://www.ecovolunteer.org

*Fielding's Volunteer Groups Links*
http://www.fieldingtravel.com/linkfinder/VolunteerGroupLinks.html
Fielding's Volunteer Groups Links provides valuable links to the world's voluntary organisations.

*Friends of the Earth*
http://www.foe.co.uk
Friends of the Earth Trust is an environmental charity which commissions detailed research and provides extensive information and educational materials and is represented in 58 countries.

*Frontier*
http://www.frontierprojects.ac.uk
Here you can find a selection of conservation projects in Africa and the Far East.

*iAgora*
http://www.iagora.com/iwork/jobdatabase/volunteering.html
You can search for volunteer opportunities in a specific country through this site.

*i-i International Projects*
http://www.i-to-i.com
Enjoy an unforgettable travel experience as an i-i volunteer through selected placements in twelve countries. For example, you can teach English, conserve the environment or work in media, medical or marketing.

*International Voluntary Service*
http://www.ivsgbn.demon.co.uk/index.html
IVS places hundreds of volunteers on work camps throughout the year, all over the world.

*One World*
http://www.oneworld.org
Jobs and volunteer work in development and global justice organisations are offered through this web site.

*Overseas Development Institute*
http://www.odi.org.uk

*Oxfam*
http://www.oxfam.org.uk/index.html

*Save the Children*
http://www.savethechildren.org

*Skillshare Africa*
http://www.skillshare.org
'Working for sustainable development.'

*United Nations Association International Service (UNAIS)*
http://www.oneworld.org/is

*United Nations Development Programme (UNDP)*
http://www.undp.org/

Y | INFO REQUEST

Teach
Primary
Secondary
Language Institutes
Universities
Monasteries

Conserve
Rainforests
Turtles

Work
Journalism
Design
IT
Medical Placements
Media
TV

# The global jobs market............................................

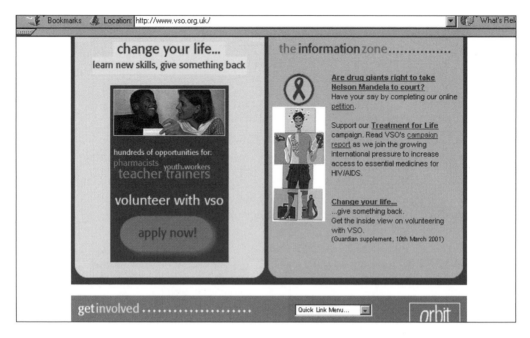

Fig. 11. VSO is one of the oldest-established international voluntary programmes, which is now open to people of almost all ages and working backgrounds.

*VOIS*
http://www.vois.org.uk
This site hosts a number of charity and voluntary organisations sites. You can browse by sector, A-Z listing or keyword.

*Voluntary Service Overseas*
http://www.vso.org.uk
You can access overseas voluntary work projects through this site.

*Voluntary Work Information Service*
http://www.workingabroad.com
Looking for environmental and humanitarian work abroad? Then this Switzerland-based organisation could be a place to start if you're looking for voluntary work projects in over 150 countries worldwide. VWIS was established in early 1997 as an independent non-profit organisation. It offers opportunities in social and community development, environment and nature conservation, human rights, wildlife surveying and expeditions, medicine and health care, construction, sanitation, housing, education and teaching, agriculture and organic farming. There are some useful links to similar organisations worldwide. Be patient, the pages can be slow to load.

*Voluntary Work*
http://www.voluntarywork.org
The purpose of this international web site is to list the world's voluntary work organisations, with feedback from those who have been to give you the best possible and easily accessible information. It includes a database of hundreds of voluntary work and community service vacancies.

*Voluntary Work Abroad Links*
http://www.usitcampus.co.uk/work/volwork.htm
You can access several links to voluntary work abroad through this page.

*Voluntary Work Overseas*
http://www.fedora.csu.ac.uk/student/cidd/specials/abroad/Volorgs.htm
Information and links for voluntary work overseas.

*Volunteer for Peace International Workcamps*
http://www.vfp.org
VFP provides programmes where people can work together to help over-come the need, violence and environmental decay we face today.

*World Service Enquiry*
http://www.wse.org.uk
WSE provides information and advice about working or volunteering overseas in the developing world for peace, justice, development or mission.

Visit the free Internet HelpZone at
**www.internet-handbooks.co.uk**
Helping you master the internet

# 3 Landing the right job

**In this chapter we will explore:**

▶ *your job search strategy*
▶ *your job search checklist*
▶ *what to include in your CV*
▶ *CVs and scanning*
▶ *creating online CVs*
▶ *electronic job applications*
▶ *sending your CV by email*
▶ *sending your CV by post*
▶ *succeeding at interviews*
▶ *your employment conditions checklist*
▶ *careers services*

## Your job search strategy

*Researching the market*
You will need to research the economics and labour market trends of the country where you would like to work, as well as the kind of skills and knowledge they are seeking. Issues such as the impact of local and national government budgets within your chosen country and region may affect the economic flow and therefore your chances of employment. Be aware of the developmental progress of your work speciality in these countries.

*Networking*
To quote that old adage, it's not what you know, but who you know, that matters most. The right information, the best resources and the strongest support are all needed to keep you focused in any jobsearch strategy. Ask yourself what are your career goals for the next six to twelve months – what do you need to achieve them? Who can help you achieve them?

*Assembling your employment package*
You will need to gather together:

(a) Copies of degrees and certificates.

(b) Letters of introduction or sponsorship (any contacts abroad are invaluable).

(c) CV.

(d) Photograph of yourself.

(e) References from previous employers.

*Applying by telephone*

When you telephone a company, either in response to an advert or on spec, your chances of selling yourself will depend on how well your character and enthusiasm come across in your voice. Speak firmly and clearly in an enthusiastic manner (smiling helps) and don't suppress your body language. Try standing up while on the phone if you want to feel more authoritative. Listen with your right ear to absorb facts and your left ear for extra intuition and listen to the tone and pitch of their voice for hidden meaning.

*Writing covering letters*

A covering letter is used when sending off your CV or an application form for a specifically advertised vacancy. Pointers to bear in mind:

1.  Put your full address and telephone number (including the country code for the UK) in the letter.

2.  Ideally address your letter to a named person if stated in the advert, if there is no name put 'Dear Sir/Madam'.

3.  If you address the letter to a named person, sign off 'Yours sincerely'. If you address the letter 'Dear Sir/Madam, sign off 'Yours faithfully'.

4.  The first paragraph of the letters should state what you are replying to, and where and when seen.

5.  The second paragraph is your sales pitch outlining your relevant skills, strengths and experience.

6.  The third paragraph is where you indicate your availability for interview and say that you have enclosed your CV.

7.  Whenever you enclose something else in an envelope, other than the letter, always put ENC. at the bottom left hand corner of your letter.

*Writing speculative letters*

Speculative letters are a form of cold-calling. They are written to companies with the intention of finding work – only not directly asking for a job. There are four good reasons for writing speculative letters.

1.  When replying to an advertised vacancy, you may be one of fifty or more applicants. When you write a spec letter, you may be one of two or three people doing the same thing.

2.  Your spec letter may arrive when a vacancy needs filling but is not yet advertised (only a very small percentage of vacancies are filled through advertisements).

3.  Your spec letter is likely to show initiative and could be placed on file for the next suitable vacancy to arise.

4.  You are so good at selling yourself that you create a need for your services.

A speculative letter is a business proposition and the aim is to get a meeting. So you need to customise each letter by researching the organisation, targeting the letter at a named individual, and identifying where you fit in. The first paragraph of the letter should state who you are, what you do and why you are writing. The second paragraph is your sales pitch containing relevant skills, strengths and experience. The third paragraph is where you request a meeting and indicate the enclosed resume.

▶ *Tip* – Write correspondence in the language of your employer, not your own. Include an SAE and an International Reply Coupon (available from Post Offices).

### Your jobsearch checklist

1.  Choose the country you want to work in.

2.  Find out as much as possible about the country, both in general and the employment situation.

3.  Choose what type of work you want to do.

4.  Ask yourself what qualifications you need for this type of work.

5.  Compile a relevant and concise employment package.

6.  Identify as many prospective employers as you can.

7.  Get your employment package translated if necessary.

8.  Write to as many employers as possible (with a SAE and relevant number of International Reply Coupons).

9.  Learn the language of your target country.

### What to include in your CV

Your CV is your sales document – selling you to prospective employees. It should be no longer than 2 pages and word-processed on light coloured, quality paper. Individually target each CV for the vacancy you are applying for. In the first quarter of the first page, include 2 or 3 separate sections detailing an area of expertise relevant to the work you are applying for. Within each section detail your accomplishments and abilities. Put your degree or other qualification(s) near the top of your CV. This is what to include:

1.  Your full name.

2.  If you don't have much of a work history, put your personal profile details at the top after your name (although this refers traditionally to paid work, consider unpaid work skills and knowledge and other skills and qualities you have gained).

3.  Your full address and postcode.
4.  Your telephone number and STD code (including the country code for the UK) date of birth.
5.  Your professional training (where and when – qualifications gained – relate your qualifications to the equivalents in the country you are applying to).
6.  Your employment history (include work experience, placements, holiday work – for gaps in employment history put down the years rather than specific months and put something like 'unemployed but working in a voluntary capacity' or 'unemployed but took a course in learning German').
7.  Your hobbies (making them relevant to the position you are seeking without bending the truth too much – add club membership or any positions of responsibility you have had as part of your interests).
8.  Other information may include driving licence, languages, community activities, smoker or non-smoker, able to work unsociable hours.
9. Two references (teacher, tutor, minister, doctor, youth worker, previous employer, a professional person).

*Things to mention*

▶ All work-related foreign travel.

▶ Successful track record abroad.

▶ Language ability.

▶ Achievements especially in foreign environments.

▶ Specialised work-related knowledge.

You will need a portfolio of CVs, each targeted at specific areas of work. You also need to bear in mind that your CV will be sent via various methods such as electronic mail or snail–mail.

*Things you should do with your CV*

Use A4 paper.
Use 10 or 12-point type size.
Keep your page margins to a minimum of 1/2' or more (1' is best, 3/4' is also preferred to 1/2').
Make your CV as legible as possible, using a non-serif type font (it is easier to scan).
Include a permanent contact, present address and phone number and STD code (including the country code for the UK), and an email address (if you have one) near the top of the first page of your CV. That will enable firms to contact you even after you have moved from your present address.
Include your job discipline(s) near your name at the top of page one of your CV and a job title for each assignment.
Include a summary paragraph near the top of your CV.
Include pertinent education and/or training.
List jobs in reverse chronological order (most current first).
Include only necessary personal information

Type 'Under contract to' for any contract assignments you may have had.

Include total number of year's experience.

Give security status, if any. If your security clearance has expired, include the date of expiration.

Write job descriptions in easy-to-understand terms. Be brief but be as complete as practical.

Include your name and page number on each page of a multiple page résumé (except no number on first page).

*Things you should not do with your CV*

Don't include your Social Security Number.

Don't exaggerate your experience.

Don't show salary or pay information.

Don't offer explanations for leaving prior employers.

Don't use abbreviations (except those that are acceptable in the engineering/technical fields, such as IBM, DBA, CAD, E/M, etc).

## CVs and scanning

If you are preparing a CV for scanning via OCR software, bear in mind the following:

1. Don't use unusual or stylised fonts in paper CVs that may potentially be scanned – use a plain standard font such as Arial or Times New Roman.

2. Use a font size of 10 point or greater.

3. Don't fold your CV but send it in a full-sized A4 envelope because folded paper sometimes does not scan well.

4. Place your name on its own at the top of each page.

5. Avoid effects such as bullets, bold, italics, underlining and graphics.

6. Provide a laser printed original copy.

7. Do not staple sheets together.

8. Save your word-processed CV as a plain text or ASCII file.

9. Use white paper and black ink.

10. All letters should be of the same quality (no light or broken letters, no smudgy or filled-in letters, etc.).

11. Don't hand write anything on your résumé.

12. If you are using a dot matrix or inkjet printer, utilise the best quality of type the printer provides (letter quality, dark copy, etc.).

13. Avoid boxes or unusual configurations.

14. Don't use columns.

Employers who use automated CV selection often use scanning software to search for words reflecting key skills including industry jargon.

You need to elaborate and specify your key words. Note that especially in the IT field, skills such as Unix or network management may be specifically searched for. So include everything you think may be relevant to the post for which you are applying.

### Creating online CVs

There are many internet resources for creating online CVs. One of the best ones is:

http://www.jobsearch.co.uk

Fig. 12. Jobsearch is one of several careers sites which will help you produce and publish your online CV.

This allows you to create CVs that can be accessed by UK employers using the JobSearch database. Another site worth visiting is http://www.monsterboard.com This is a good source of vacancies as well as being able to access their CV Builder page to complete a pro-forma CV or to submit your own. *Note:* some organisations charge a fee for their CV-building service.

### Electronic job applications

Electronic applications are those that employ any sort of computer method in the recruitment process and might include the following:

1. You might be asked to apply directly to the organisation using e-mail. Many organisations now offer the chance for you to 'post your CV on the web'. This means entering it into the database of an organisation that will either try actively to get you a job or will passively allow an employer to interrogate their database and select you for interview from your CV details.

2. Some companies ask you to put your application onto a diskette.

3. Other types of electronic methods of getting work involve Usenet newsgroups. Some of these are dedicated to recruitment and may have titles such as jobs.offered and jobs.wanted. You can send your details to such newsgroups or apply for posts you see advertised on them.

4. You might send a paper CV to a company that then uses Optical Character Recognition (OCR) software to scan it into the computer database (see previous section).

5. You may decide to publish your own web site on the internet that contains information about yourself and your CV.

Some employers and recruitment agencies allow you to apply for jobs by completing an on-screen form. Employers and agencies may use standard searches to find candidates. These often rely on finding specific key words in the descriptions of your various activities so make sure you use positive, active words that are appropriate to the type of work for which you are applying.

## Sending your CV by email

You could send your CV as a formatted document in an attachment to your email message. However, you may run the risk of their email system not being able to handle your attachment. You need to send your application in a format which can be read by any computer and this means using ASCII code (American Standard Code for Information Interchange). If you were to send it as an email attachment in Word, the receiving company's computer might translate it automatically into a garbled mess. You can type it into your word processor rather than use the text message part of your email tool, but if you do, you need to remember the following:

1. Use a monospaced font such as Courier. Other proportionally spaced fonts change accordingly when you convert them and alter any tab settings you have used creating a mess – you cannot use bold or italic type in ASCII.

2. You cannot use special indents or margin adjustments, although you can use ordinary tabs and spacing.

3. Keep individual lines to fewer than 70 characters wide. The receiving computer may have different screen widths and email tools which will create a garbled mess out of anything wider than 70 characters. You can create some interest in the document by using hyphens, asterisks and the letter 'o' for bullet points.

4. Save your file in ASCII by opening the File menu and using the Save As option, name your file and save it as a Text Only file if you are using Word.

5. You can send it as an attachment in your email tool by specifying the

directory it is in on the hard drive or you can paste it into the text message area and send it as you would a normal email message

If you want to email your CV, clarify whether you need to send it in the main body of the text or as an attachment. Bear in mind when sending your CV in the main body of an email what your viewer will see first on their screen – start your CV with a career summary or employment objective and put contact details at the end. Don't forget to send a covering letter, just as you would in print, unless you are instructed not to do so by the receiving organisation.

## Sending your CV by post

You can also post your CV to one of the 'jobs.wanted' newsgroups or the 'misc.jobs.resumes' newsgroups. The former tends to be related to an area of work and the latter cover any work and any country. A recent *Tomorrow's World* programme on the BBC suggested that around 15 major companies are using this method in the UK. It is far more common in the USA and observers believe that it will grow in popularity here. See page 64 for more on newsgroups.

When posting a CV to a CV bank or employment agency database, you need to be clear about the kind of work you are looking for. A CV format will have to be completed that is the same for everyone. Employers will use key words to select CVs they want to look at further.

▶ *Check* – Do you need to have your employment package translated into the language of your potential employer?

## Succeeding at interviews

*Interview facts*
An interview or a business meeting is your chance to sell yourself. Did you know that:

1.  55 per cent of your success will depend on visual factors

2.  38 per cent of your success will depend on your voice.

3.  7 per cent of your success will depend on your spoken word.

▶ *Key point* – Your success (or otherwise) will be determined within the first 3 minutes of your entering the room.

The interview is your opportunity to sell yourself directly to a company. You will be asked questions and maybe given some tasks to do. Answer the questions as fully as you can without waffling. Think of the answers that they are likely to be looking for and provide them, together with examples of your related skills and knowledge. Show them by illustration what you can do and what you know. And remember, you have as much right to ask questions of any prospective employer as they do of you.

# Landing the right job ............................................

*Essential interview tips*

1. Prepare – prepare – prepare.

2. Research the company and know what the position is about.

3. Provide working examples of what you know and what you can do.

4. Provide working examples of relevant achievements.

5. Show how you can solve their problems.

6. Have the confidence to be yourself.

7. Ask intelligent questions.

8. Be enthusiastic without going overboard.

9. Looking the interviewer/panel in the eye with a smile.

10. Sit upright and relaxed in the chair.

11. Think professionally – behave professionally.

12. Remember that you can vote with your feet – you might not like what they are offering.

## Your employment conditions checklist

This list gives you some idea of what you need to check before accepting an offer of work abroad, although it isn't exhaustive:

1. What are the full contact details of your employer?

2. Will your employer meet the cost of travel out from the UK for your family as well as yourself?

3. Will your eventual return to the UK as well as your departure be taken care of?

4. What are the accommodation arrangements?

5. Will the employer subsidise or pay for you and your family's hotel bills for a reasonable period until you find somewhere to live?

6. If social security payments are higher than in the UK, will your employer make up the difference?

7. Will they contribute to your medical expenses if free medical attention is not available or inadequate?

8. If your salary is paid in sterling, are you protected against loss of local buying power in case of devaluation?

9. Is your salary indexed-linked to the cost of living?

10. Would your employer contribute towards language teaching for you and your partner?

11. Who is going to pay for domestic utilities (electricity, phone etc)?

12. Where exactly will you be working?

13. What is your job title?

14. What are your responsibilities?

15. Who are you answerable to?

16. When do you start your contract and how long will it last?

17. Is the contract renewable?

18. Is there a probationary period?

19. What is your net salary, how often is it paid and how is it paid?

20. How many hours a week will you work?

21. Is there provision for paid leave?

22. Is there provision for sickness leave?

23. How much notice does either side have to give to terminate the contract?

24. What extras can you expect?

25. Which country's laws are this contract governed by, for example, the UK or the country of work?

26. Is the legal status of your employment clear?

27. Have all the terms of the job and provision of your remuneration been confirmed in writing?

## Careers services

The following sites deal with career services on all levels including general career development, occupational information, CV design, interview skills and networking.

*1st-Impact*
http://www.1st-imp.com
This site offers résumé-writing, employment, and career management resources. Check the jobsearch area, the career café, career news, the gold mine, reading room, career counsellor and bookstore.

*A Better Career*
http://www.abc.vg
Here you can find some hard-hitting and useful articles for anyone interested in advancing their career.

*Alec's Free CV, Job Hunting & Interview Tips*
http://www.alec.co.uk
This site offers common-sense advice for jobseekers. The services range from getting a foot in the door to careers guidance. There is also the offer of a professional CV-writing service.

## CV Special

▶ Home
▶ CV Special service
▶ A bad CV
▶ A good CV
▶ Impact
▶ Letters
▶ Case histories
▶ Write your own CV
▶ Read more
▶ Free CV appraiser
▶ Priority CV Appraisal
▶ Order CV Services

# Landing the right job ...............................................

Fig. 13. Alec's CV and career tips could help you land the job you want.

*Bradley CVs*
http://www.bradleycvs.co.uk
On this site you can pay for a professionally written CV and get advice on seeking and securing jobs. There are also plenty of links to recruitment sites.

*Buzzword Career Management*
http://www.buzzwordcv.com
This company offers a broad range of services to assist managing and developing careers.

*CareerBuilder*
http://www.careerbuilder.com
This site provides advice on résumé writing (including electronic ones), links to career information, features and career management tools.

*Careers Gateway*
http://www.careersoft.co.uk
With links to the web sites of professional bodies, universities and a host of sites to help with job seeking, you should start your career surfing here. Careers teachers and advisers will also find useful teaching ideas and resources.

*Career Guide*
http://www.careerguide.net
The Career Guide is a resource directory of online career related service providers for consumers and corporate visitors.

42

*CareerLab*
http://www.careerlab.com
This is the site of a career and human resources consulting firm. Their product line includes career counselling, management testing and assessment, executive coaching, performance improvement, 360-degree reviews, team building, and outplacement. A feature of the site is its collection of ready-made cover letters.

*CareerMatch*
http://www.intec.edu.za/career/career.htm
CareerMatch is a quick way to get free, personal vocational guidance. All you do is fill out a form that involves the ranking of various describing words. You submit your form online and within seconds you receive your personal CareerMatch results. When you submit your questionnaire to INTEC for evaluation, the CareerMatch programme is able to determine a unique profile in terms of six of your most significant characteristics or personality attributes. Using this profile, it compares and matches it against similar profiles established for about 100 different careers.

*CareerNet*
http://www.uea.ac.uk/ccen/details/overseas.htm
There are several useful links for working abroad from this page maintained at the University of East Anglia.

*Career Resource Centre*
http://www.careers.org
From the home page, you can link into jobs, employer directories, learning resources, home office resources and career services.

*CareerSign*
http://www.careersign.com
CareerSign is a rich resource of research-based advice, guidance and information to help individuals to improve their career management skills.

*Career Solutions*
http://www.careersolutions.co.uk
You will find this a user-friendly, detailed site including advice about CVs and interviews, and job listings links.

| Career Help |
| --- |
| **How to Be Wanted** |
| **Outstanding CV's** |
| **Personal Marketing** |
| **Interview Skills** |
| **Career Management** |

*Careers Information and Guidance on the Web*
http://www.aiuto.net/uk.htm
This is a 60-page guide to more than 400 British web sites dedicated to job search, the professions, schools, vocational training, universities and research.

*Careers Portal*
http://www.careers-portal.co.uk
Links to jobs, careers advice and services, universities, schools and colleges are all to be found on this UK search directory.

# Landing the right job ·············································

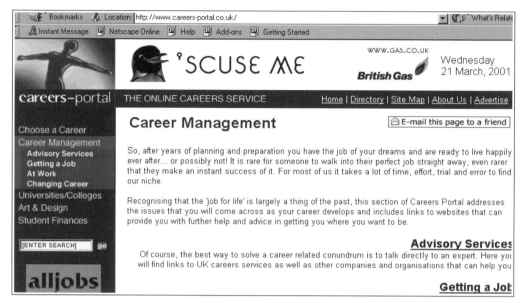

Fig. 14. Check the Careers Portal for help with your job hunt.

*Careers Research and Advisory Centre*
http://www.crac.org.uk
CRAC is an independent development agency that supports lifelong learning and career development and offers expertise, information and access to a national network.

*CareerWorld*
http://www.careerworld.net
This site offers a free service to people about to leave school, college or university in the UK. It provides detailed career advice, job vacancies, vocational guidance and gap-year choices together with university and college opportunities at both further and higher education.

*Career-Zone UK*
http://www.careerzone-uk.com
This site offers impartial advice and information on all aspects of career, employment, education and training advice in the UK. Visit the library, bookshop and careers clinic. See the features page and access over 5,000 vacancies.

*CV Special*
http://www.cvspecial.co.uk
CV Special is a site well worth visiting. It oozes expertise and professionalism and gives users a great deal of free and very useful hints and guidelines on getting their CV and covering letters right.

*Employment Overseas*
http://www.shef.ac.uk/ ~ cas/students/rainbow/rainii.html
This page aims to provide a general overview of some of the sources of information held by the Sheffield University Careers Service on overseas employment.

*Glasgow University Careers Services*
http://www.gla.ac.uk/otherdepts/careers
This site includes careers services, links, vacation and part-time work, industrial placements, overseas opportunities, postgraduate study and funding and graduates recruiters.

*Heriot-Watt University Careers Services*
http://www.hw.ac.uk/careers
This site links to both UK and international web sites for careers and employment, recruiter's home pages, vacancies, job-hunting skills and careers information.

*Internet SourceBook Career Centre*
http://www.internetsourcebook.com/jobs/index.html
This site provides a source of newsgroups containing details of jobs in the UK, Europe, USA, Canada, Russia and Australia. It provides profiles of over 500 internet companies that are now hiring, including links to their job opportunity web pages. Check out the CareerSeek résumé and job-listing system. You can post your résumé and search the job listings.

*JobBank USA*
http://www.jobbankusa.com
JobBank USA specialises in providing career information including job and résumé database services to job candidates, employers and recruitment firms both in the USA and worldwide.

*Job Hunting Abroad*
http://www.labourmobility.com/job_hunting_abroad.htm
Here you can find helpful tips on finding work in other countries including

Fig. 15. The Labourmobility web site can help you if you are Europe-bound.

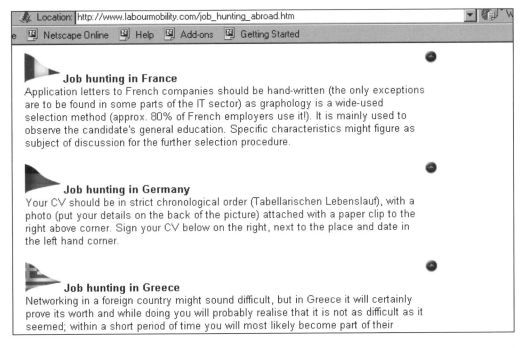

CV tips. The site offers information on cultural management differences, occasional newsletters, publications, European labour market information, checklist for planning to work abroad, questionnaire on 'successful expatriate skills' (for printing) and links to key European labour market information sites.

*Job Interview Network*
http://www.job-interview.net
A fascinating site featuring job interview tips, questions and answers (related to over 40 professions and job functions) plus sample interview questions.

*Monster Board UK*
http://www.monster.co.uk
This version is the UK offspring of the original US Monster Board and offers a variety of career services.

*Professional CVs and Résumés*
http://www.edinburghconcepts.com/cv_homepage.htm
This site offers free CV and résumé tips plus interview resources, job links and more.

*University of Leeds Careers Services*
http://www.leeds.ac.uk/careers/othelink/overseas.htm
The site contains some useful links for working overseas.

*Virtual Careers Library*
http://www.kcl.ac.uk/kis/college/careers/links/links.htm
This is a site hosted by Kings College London Career Services on behalf of the University of London Careers Service. There are links to career choices, further study, job-hunting resources, regional and international working, self employment, voluntary and vacation work and employer web sites.

## More Internet Handbooks to help you

*Careers Guidance on the Internet*, by Laurel Alexander.
*Finding a Job on the Internet*, Brendan Murphy (2nd edition).

# 4 Moving overseas

**In this chapter we will explore:**

▶ *foreign currency*
▶ *tax*
▶ *social security*
▶ *insurance*
▶ *motoring*
▶ *health precautions*
▶ *travel documents*
▶ *home comforts*
▶ *translation and languages*
▶ *relocation services*

Members of the European Community (EC) have the right to live and work in other member states (Belgium, Denmark, Greece, Republic of Ireland, France, West Germany, Italy, Luxembourg, Netherlands, Spain and Portugal) without a work permit. UK nationals working in another member state have the same rights as nationals of that country as to salary, working conditions, training, social security and housing.

The Overseas Placing Unit (OPU) is a division of the Employment Services and can be contacted at your local Jobcentre. It has access to overseas vacancies held on the national vacancy system, and the Oracle Jobfinder system. If you wish to find work outside of the EC, the OPU can give advice but there is no current system for exchange of applications between the UK and these countries. These vacancies will be handled by recruitment agencies.

## Foreign currency

*Bank of England's Euro Page*
http://www.bankofengland.co.uk/euro/index.htm
Practical advice can be found here for businesses and financiers concerning the introduction of the single European currency.

*Travel-Finder's Currency Converter*
http://www.travel-finder.com/convert/convert.htm
You can use the calculator in a pop-up window to work out all your foreign currency requirements.

*Universal Currency Converter*
http://www.xe.net/ucc/
The site offers interactive foreign exchange rate conversion. XE.com's Universal Currency Converter made its debut in May of 1995. Not only was it one of the very first useful financial information services on the web, it was one of the first interactive web services ever to appear. Today, it is independently ranked as the world's most popular internet

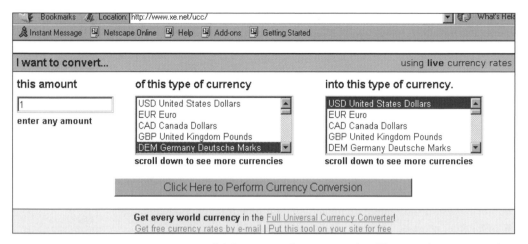

Fig. 16. The Universal Currency Converter is a neat way of checking the local cost of goods and services in just about any foreign currency.

currency tool. It has grown from supporting 12 currencies to supporting over 180, from over 250 geographical locations.

## Taxation for expats

The organisation that recruits you should be able to help you with regard to your tax position both abroad and in the UK. Working abroad could be an excellent opportunity to pay less tax on your earnings and investments. To find out more:

1. Contact the Inland Revenue, which produces various leaflets on the tax aspects of working and living abroad.

2. Seek advice from a specialist adviser in expatriate finance.

3. Read current books on personal finance for expatriates.

4. Contact your professional membership organisation if you belong to one.

5. Contact your bank.

Here are some key web sites on taxation for expats:

*Ernst & Young World Tax*
http://www.doingbusinessin.com
Ernst & Young's popular tax library offers a wealth of tax and business knowledge in more than 140 countries, updated quarterly. There are links to doing business around the world, corporate tax, and the global executive.

*HM Customs and Excise Home Page*
http://www.hmce.gov.uk

*Inland Revenue (UK)*
http://www.inlandrevenue.gov.uk
Provides some general guidance about the rules of residency and domicile for tax purposes.

*Lowtax Net*
http://www.lowtax.net/
Lowtax Net is a complete international taxation resource for professionals and investors.

*Tax-News*
http://www.tax-news.com
This UK-based site offers articles on offshore tax, and ecommerce, legal, political, and economic news relating to taxes.

*Taxup*
http://www.taxup.com
This is a really detailed guide to worldwide tax rates, plus business and legal news for expats and offshore investors. Recommended.

*Web Directory: UK Taxation Directory*
http://www.uktax.demon.co.uk
Here is a useful portal site of UK taxation resources on the internet, plus an email directory of UK tax professionals.

The global di

**Useful tools**

Currency Converter
Anonymous Web Surfing
Map An Address
Free SMS Worldwide
Corporateinformation.com
Phone Directories
World Weather Forecasts
Translate Anything
Dictionary
World Time
Currency site
Tax Treaty Database

## Social security

The following pages contain information and help on *Going Abroad Benefits* published by the UK Department of Social Security

*Child Benefit*
http://www.dss.gov.uk/ba/GBI/5a6b5e4.htm
This contains information regarding child benefit in the case of temporary or permanent absence from the UK.

*Earnings Top Up*
http://www.dss.gov.uk/ba/GBI/5a6d247.htm
The page contains information regarding earnings top-up for temporary and permanent absences.

*Housing*
http://www.dss.gov.uk/ba/GBI/5a6bcf2.htm
This explains about housing benefit for temporary and permanent absences.

*Incapacity Benefit*
http://www.dss.gov.uk/ba/GBI/5a6c0fa.htm
The page contains information regarding incapacity benefit for temporary and permanent absences.

*Income Support / Jobseekers Allowance*
http://www.dss.gov.uk/ba/GBI/5a6c1fc.htm
Here you can find out about income support/jobseekers allowance for temporary and permanent absences.

*Maternity Allowance*
http://www.dss.gov.uk/ba/GBI/5a6c481.htm
The page contains information regarding maternity allowance for temporary and permanent absence.

*Reduced Earnings Allowance*
http://www.dss.gov.uk/ba/GBI/5a6c8df.htm
You can find out here about the reduced earnings allowance for temporary and permanent absence.

*Unemployability Supplement*
http://www.dss.gov.uk/ba/GBI/5a6cb8f.htm
Information regarding unemployability supplement for temporary and permanent absence.

## Insurance

Consider what insurance you may need to arrange, such as personal liability, medical expenses, strikes and delays, personal accident, cancellation and loss of baggage and money.

*British Expats*
http://britishexpats.com
This is an excellent resource for insurance and other financial advice for UK expats, along with news and many other practical features.

*Expat Financial*
http://www.expatfinancial.com
The firm provides international life, health and disability insurance and investment products for individual expatriates living abroad and their employers. It brokers insurance and financial plans designed for expatriates of any nationality.

*Medibroker International*
http://www.medibroker.com
Medibroker is a private medical insurer specialising in policies for UK citizens who are living or working abroad.

*Morgan Price International Healthcare*
http://www.morgan-price.com
This is a company offering medical, travel and accident insurance to UK residents and those living or working abroad.

## Motoring

If your new employer isn't providing you with a company car, look into the possibilities of buying a car in the country of your work, taking your own vehicle, or buying a new vehicle in the UK and shipping it out. See also:

*The Automobile Association (AA)*
http://www.theaa.com

*Driving Permit*
http://www.drivingpermit.co.uk
An international driving permit (IDP) is an internationally recognised, low-cost document which, when accompanied by your own UK licence, will allow you to drive a private motor vehicle in a foreign country. This site has been set up as a free information source.

## Health precautions

▶ *Check* – Will you need vaccinations for your chosen country?

*Department of Health (UK)*
http://www.doh.gov.uk
This is an enormous portal site to UK-based health information and resources.

*MASTA*
http://www.masta.org
The Medical Advisory Services for Travellers Abroad was set up in 1984 at the London School of Hygiene and Tropical Medicine. It offers health and travel information for travelling abroad and covers diseases, immunisations, travel products, visas, and insurance. Its services range from the supply of vaccines and travel medicines to research on important travel issues and the development of unique products for travellers.

Fig. 17. MASTA, the London-based Medical Advisory Service for Travellers Abroad.

## Travel documents

▶ *Passports* – Make sure that your passport is up to date, and that its expiry date covers the expected length of your overseas stay by any margin that may be required.

▶ *Visas and work permits* – As a UK citizen you don't need visas for EC member states, some USA and certain Eastern bloc countries. Visas can be obtained from the relevant foreign embassy, usually in London. Some EC member states countries don't require a work permit for residents of the UK. In some countries you can only get a work permit if you are taking up a permanent job that has been arranged before you arrive. The temporary worker may find work permits are a stumbling block.

*Ambler Collins*
http://www.amblercollins.com
The site offers advice about working abroad and how to obtain a working visa for major destinations such as the USA and Australia.

*BCL Immigration Services*
http://www.visa-free.com
London-based BCL operates this excellent web site which outlines visa requirements worldwide.

*Columbus World Travel Guide*
http://www.worldtravelguide.net/navigate/world.asp
Visit this site for a general guide to visas, passports, currency, health, resorts, transport and accommodation covering the world.

*Travel Document Systems*
http://www.traveldocs.com/ke/
This site gives access to assistance in procuring visas and other travel documents covering Africa, Asia, Australia, Europe and America.

*United Kingdom Passport Agency*
http://www.ukpa.gov.uk

Fig. 18. The web site of the UK Passport Agency.

Remember to check out the UK Government Passport Agency web site for information and guidance.

*Visa-Free List*
http://www.bclimser.demon.co.uk/bclvisjr.htm
Visa-Free is an unmoderated discussion list covering problems associated with international travel, and in particular how to acquire a
different nationality to overcome these problems. Visa-Free can be
accessed by anyone wanting information on visa-free travel, or who
wants useful tips about gaining another nationality quickly.

*US Visas and Immigration*
http://www.us-visas.co.uk
These US emigration consultants offer complete visa services for obtaining work permits and 'green cards' for the United States.

## Home comforts

*Brits Abroad*
http://www.britsabroad.co.uk/
This is a virtual corner shop where you can get supplies of such com-
modities as HP sauce, Marmite, tea, coffee, baked beans, Farley's rusks,
Jaffa Cakes, Ambrosia creamed rice and more.

*Back in Blighty*
http://www.backinblighty.com
The site offers all kinds of resources that a British expat might need, ran-
ging from gardening links to cricket scores.

## Translation and languages

Here are web sites which offer translation services, or which can help
you to learn another language. A working knowledge of the language
of your host country (if not English) is possibly the most valuable skill
you can acquire, and one which could transform your whole overseas
experience.

*Berlitz*
http://www.berlitz.com
Check out the language instruction and translations facilities of one of
the world's leading language schools and language book publishers.

*Foreign Language for Travellers*
If you need to communicate with people in another language you may
find the following sites useful:

> http://travlang.com/languages/index.html
> http://babelfish.altavista.com/translate.dyn

*Freedict.com*
http://www.freedict.com/
This site offers a word for word translation service. You will find online
dictionaries from English to Afrikaans, Danish, Dutch, Finnish, French,
Hungarian, Indonesian, Italian, Japanese, Norwegian, Portuguese, Russian, Spanish and Swedish.

# Moving overseas.............................................................

*G and W*
http://www.g-and-w.co.uk/
Through this site you can access translation and copywriting specialists in Eastern languages, including Arabic, Japanese, Chinese, Korean, Hebrew, Russian, Greek, and Indian languages.

*Institute of Translating and Interpreting*
http://www.iti.org.uk/
You can access the ITI's online directory of translators and interpreters from here.

*Language Today*
http://shop.logos.it/language.today/
Here is an online magazine for everyone working in applied languages – translators, interpreters, terminologists, lexicographers and technical writers.

*Languages for Business Communication*
http://www.lfbc.com/lfbc/start.htm
You can find foreign language training for business people through this site – French, German, Spanish, Italian, Dutch, Portuguese, Japanese and Russian, plus translation services.

*Language International*
http://www.language-international.com
This is a magazine for language professionals.

*Latin American Language Services*
http://www.lals.co.uk/home.htm
LALS a UK specialist in Latin American languages – Spanish & Portuguese. It helps British companies and individuals with tuition, translation and interpretation.

*Mike Ellis Communications*
http://homepages.nationwideisp.net/ ~ mike.ellis/
This is the home page of an independent consultant specialising in presentation design and management, with a Swedish/English translation service.

*Spanish-English Translation*
http://www.spanishtranslator.org/
This site offers a wealth of information and resources for translators, people interested in the Spanish and English languages, and for anyone who needs translation services.

*Technolingua*
http://www.vsl.co.uk/tecnolingua/
TecnoLingua offers a high-quality translation and interpreting service in all language combinations.

## Relocation services

*Baxters International Removals*
http://www.baxters-intl.co.uk
Baxters are long-standing members of the British Association of Removers.

*Bishop's Move*
http://www.bishops-move.co.uk
Bishop's Move has been helping people move their homes and business for more than 140 years. It has a nationwide network of branch offices, and a staff of more than 350. It can move specialist items such as antiques, IT equipment, industrial machinery or even complete libraries. Its services encompass record management, confidential shredding, and porterage. For international shipping, it offers a complete day-to-day service for moves to Europe and all other parts of the world.

*Brewer and Turnbull*
http://www.mrmover.co.uk
This is another household name when it comes to moving, whether you want to go just a few miles or relocate halfway around the world. It claims to be the largest post-war shipper of household goods to many overseas destinations, and to have pioneered containerised storage in the UK. It is a national company with branches throughout the country.

*Burke Bros*
http://www.burkebros.co.uk
Burke Brothers is a leading UK removal company, experienced in international moves of household goods and company property to destinations like Australia, New Zealand, Canada, the United States, South Africa and the countries of central and south America and the Caribbean. This site is a cut above the rest, with lots of useful information, for example on moving to different countries such as France or Ireland.

*Excess Baggage*
http://www.excess-baggage.co.uk/index.stm
This is an international removals and shipping company which can help you move your goods to any world destination.

*First Point International*
http://www.firstpointinter.com
This is the site of another worldwide relocation specialist.

*G B Liners*
http://www.gb-liners.co.uk
G B Liners offers a complete home removals service, local or long distance. It will take care of countrywide delivery of antiques, furniture, bequests, as single articles or part loads, containerised storage, the movement of pianos, musical instruments, and electronic equipment, and office removal. It offers a European road van service, overseas packing, shipping and documentation.

Fig. 19. The Excess
Baggage service.

*Pickfords*
http://www.pickfords.co.uk
Pickfords is the oldest-established removal company in the UK, tracing its history back 400 years. It has 75 branches and storage centres through-out the UK, and 1,200 worldwide, providing home movers with a local, national and international service. It can take care of gas, electricity and plumbing disconnection and reconnection, skip hire, lifting and refitting carpets, cleaning, gardening, handyman, dismantling and reassembly of garden sheds, aerials and satellite dishes, security alarms, locksmiths, and the transport of a second car, caravan or boat.

*PRS Europe*
http://www.prseurope.com
PRS is a supplier of relocation services to companies and individual expatriates. The firm has offices in Belgium and Holland.

## More Internet Handbooks to help you

*Personal Finance on the Internet*, Graham Jones.
*Travel & Holidays on the Internet*, Graham Jones.

# 5 Searching for information

**In this chapter we will explore:**

▶ *searching the internet*
▶ *tips for searching*
▶ *bookmarking your favourite web sites*
▶ *search engines and directories*
▶ *search utilities*
▶ *newsgroups and internet mailing lists*

. . . . . . . . . . . . . . . . . . . . . . . . . . . . . . . . . . . . . . . . . .

## Searching the internet

The usual way to look up something on the internet is to go to the web site of a well-known search engine or internet directory. These services are free and open to everyone.

▶ *Search engines* – These are also known as spiders or crawlers. They have highly sophisticated search tools that automatically seek out web sites across the internet. These trawl through and index literally millions of pages of internet content. As a result they often find information that is not listed in traditional directories.

▶ *Internet directories* – These are developed and compiled by people, rather than by computers. Web authors submit their web site details, and these details get listed in the relevant sections of the directory.

The browser that your ISP supplies you with – typically Internet Explorer or Netscape Navigator – will include an internet search facility, ready for you to use, but you are perfectly free to visit any of the search engines listed below, and use them yourself. America Online has its own dedicated browser and search engine.

Most people refer to internet directories as search engines and lump the two together. For the purposes of this book, we will refer to them all as search engines. Popular search engines have now become big web sites in their own right, usually combining many useful features. As well as search boxes where you can type key words to summarise what you are looking for, you will usually also find handy directories of information, news, email and many other services. There are hundreds if not thousands of search engines freely available. The biggest and best known are AltaVista, Excite, Google, Infoseek, Lycos and Yahoo! (the most popular of all).

If you are not sure where to start with search engines, you can visit one of the three sites below: they provide links to thousands of search engines and offer help on how to use them.

*List of Search Engines*
http://www.search-engine-index.co.uk
This enterprising British site offers a free list of hundreds of search

# Searching for information...........................................

engines, covering all kinds of different topics. There are software search engines, multiple search engines, email and news search engines, web search engines, commercial search engines, word reference and science search, law search, TV, film and music search, image search, technology manufacturers search, and various localised search engines.

## Latest Search Engine News

Ask Jeeves Thinking
Outside the Banner
uk.internet.com
Apr 19 2001 11:50AM

More Hoo For You -- Stone
Search Engine
Research Buzz
Apr 18 2001 11:38PM

Vodafone Taps Google
Search Engine for
Wireless Internet Portal
Mformobile
Apr 18 2001 3:17PM

Google Joins Forces With
Vodafone Global Platform

*Search Engine Colossus*
http://www.searchenginecolossus.com
Here you will find a huge collection of links to just about every search engine in the world.

*Search Engines*
http://www.dis.strath.ac.uk/business/engines.html
This page has links to individual major internet search engines, to multiple (meta) search engines, and to long lists of search engines.

## Tips for searching

1. If you want general information, try AltaVista, Google or Yahoo! first. For specific information, try one or more of the major search engines. After experimenting, many people decide on their own favourite search engine and stick to it most of the time.

2. If you do a search for expatriate finance the search engine will search for expatriate and search for finance quite separately. This could produce irrelevant details. The way to avoid this is to enclose all your key words inside a pair of quotation marks. If you type in "expatriate finance" then only web sites with that combination of words should be listed for you.

3. George Boole was a 19th-century English mathematician who worked on logic. He gave his name to Boolean operators – simple words like AND, OR and NOT. If you include these words in your searches, it should narrow down the results, for example: 'working AND abroad NOT Europe'. However, don't go overboard and restrict the search too much, or you may get few or no results.

4. Try out several different search engines, and see which one you like the best. Or you could obtain the handy little search utility called Web Ferret (see below): if the information is not on one search engine, Web Ferret can usually find it on one or more of the others.

## Bookmarking your favourite web sites

Your browser enables you to save the addresses of any web sites you specially like, and may want to revisit. These are called Bookmarks in Netscape, or Favorites in Internet Explorer (US spelling) and America Online. In either case, simply mouse-click on the relevant button on your browser's toolbar – Bookmarks or Favorites as the case may be. This produces a drop-down menu that you click on to add the site concerned. When you want to revisit that site later, click again on the same button; then click the name of the web site you bookmarked, and within a few seconds it should open for you.

## Search engines

*AltaVista*
http://www.altavista.com
http://www.altavista.co.uk
AltaVista is one of the most popular search sites among web users world wide. It contains details of millions of web pages on its massive and ever-growing database. You can either follow the trails of links from its home page, or (better) type in your own key words into its search box. You can even search in about 25 different languages. The dedicated UK page has a link to 'jobs', leading to additional links to IT and computers, job banks, job search, and working holidays. Of course you can also do you own searches for specific information.

*Ask Jeeves*
http://www.askjeeves.com
Ask Jeeves offers a slightly different approach to searches. It invites you to ask questions on the internet just as you would of a friend or colleague. For example you could type in something like: 'Where can I find out about graduate engineers?' Jeeves retrieves the information, drawing from a knowledge base of millions of standard answers.

*Electronic Yellow Pages*
http://www.eyp.co.uk
These electronic yellow pages are organised on the same lines as the paper edition. Just type in the details of the information you need – anything from careers to training – and it quickly searches for appropriate services in your local area.

*Excite*
http://www.excite.com
http://www.excite.co.uk
Excite is another of the top ten search engines and directories on the internet. To refine your search, simply click the check boxes next to the words you want to add and then click the Search Again button. There are separate Excite home pages for several different countries and cultures including Australia, Chinese, France, German, Italy, Japan, Netherlands, Spain, Sweden, and the USA. Excite, too, now has a substantial UK section, and the home page contains a link 'Find a job'. You can do company search, and explore job-hunting tips. Also, try typing in 'overseas jobs' into the search box.

*Global Online Directory*
http://www.god.co.uk
Launched in 1996, GOD is fairly unusual among search engines in that it is UK based, and aims to be a premier European search service. Features of the site include a 'global search' where you can search for web sites by country, state, province, county or even city by city, narrowing down the information for a more focused result.

# Searching for information.............................................

Fig. 20. Google
international jobsearch.

*Google*
http://www.google.com
Google has emerged as one of the top internet search facilities in the last couple of years. With its no-nonsense functional approach, it has indexed well over a billion pages on the world wide web, and is now helping to power Yahoo!

*HotBot Jobs*
http://www.hotbot.com/jobs
This is an impressive, very popular, and well-classified search engine and directory, now associated with Lycos. From this page you can link into CareerBuilder, careers pages and portals.

*Infoseek*
http://www.infoseek.co.uk
Through the UK page of this established search engine, you can access links to work, training, CV posting, vacancies, advice and recruitment agencies.

*Internet Address Finder*
http://www.iaf.net
The IAF is used by millions of web users for searching and finding the names, email addresses, and now Intel Internet videophone contacts, of other users worldwide. With millions of addresses it is one of the most comprehensive email directories on the internet. By registering, you will also enable others to find you.

*Looksmart*
http://www.looksmart.com
This is another good directory with a huge number of catalogued sites.

You can find it on the Netscape Net Search Page. If your search is not successful, you are redirected to AltaVista.

*Lycos*
http://www.lycos.com
http://www.lycos.co.uk
Founded in 1995, Lycos is another of the top ten worldwide web search engines. Lycos is the name for a type of ground spider ('spider' being the term for a type of search engine). It searches document titles, headings, links, and keywords, and returns the first few words of each page it indexes for your search. Since 1997, with the media giant Bertelsmann, it has launched Lycos sites in 11 European countries.

*Metacrawler*
http://www.metacrawler.com
MetaCrawler was originally developed by Erik Selberg and Oren Etzioni at the University of Washington, and released to the internet in 1995. In response to each user query, it incorporates results from all the top search engines. It collates results, eliminates duplication, scores the results and provides the user with a list of relevant sites.

*SavvySearch*
http://www.savvysearch.com/
Owned by CNET, SavvySearch is one of the leading providers of meta-search services. It offers a single point of access to hundreds of different search engines, guides, archives, libraries and other resources. You type in a keyword query which is then immediately sent out to all appropriate internet search engines. The results are gathered and displayed within a few seconds.

*Scoot Yahoo!*
http://scoot.yahoo.co.uk
Yahoo! has combined with the British directory Scoot to offer a search facility for people seeking UK-oriented information, businesses and organisations. Once you have found the organisation you are looking for you can click straight into their web site if they have one.

*Search.com*
http://search.cnet.com
This service is run by CNET, one of the world's leading new-media companies. From the home page you can click an A-Z list of options which displays an archive of all its search engines. The list is long, but just about everything you need to master the web is there. You can search yellow pages, phone numbers, email addresses, message boards, software downloads, and easily do all kinds of special searches.

*UK Directory*
http://www.ukdirectory.co.uk
This is a useful directory listing to UK-based web sites. You can browse it or search it. It has a well-classified subject listing. UK Directory is simple

| Lycos Services |
| --- |
| ▪ Free SMS  NEW |
| ▪ £10k to be won NEW |
| ▪ Free text messaging |
| ▪ Free Email |
| ▪ Weather |
| ▪ Lycos Chat |
| ▪ My Lycos |
| ▪ Play Games Online |
| ▪ UK Maps |
| ▪ Free Internet Access |
| ▪ Lycos Radio |
| ▪ Free Home Page |

| Lycos Partner |
| --- |
| ▪ BT |
| ▪ Loot |
| ▪ Thomson Directories |
| ▪ Travel@leisureplanet |
| ▪ Books@BOL.com |
| ▪ Mortgages with John C |

# Searching for information...........................................

and intuitive to use. You don't need to know the name of the company, service or person to find the things you are interested in. Just look in the category that best suits your needs. Use it like a telephone directory.

*UK Plus*
http://www.ukplus.co.uk
The parent company of this UK-oriented search engine and database is the Daily Mail & General Trust – owners of the *Daily Mail,* the *Mail on Sunday, London Evening Standard* and a number of UK regional newspapers – so it draws on a long tradition of publishing. It has built up a vast store of web site reviews written by a team of journalists. Although it concentrates on UK web sites, you will also find many from all over the world which are likely to be of interest to British-based readers.

*UK Yellow Web Directory*
http://www.yell.co.uk
This site is operated by the yellow pages division of British Telecom. It is indexed 'by humans' and is searchable. A number of non-UK sites are included in the database. There is also an A to Z company listing, but note that companies whose names begin with 'The' are listed under T. A Business Compass lists 'the best' business internet resources, with links and brief descriptions.

*Webcrawler*
http://webcrawler.com
Webcrawler is a fast worker and returns an impressive list of links. It analyses the full text of documents, allowing the searcher to locate key words which may have been buried deep within a document's text. Webcrawler is now part of Excite.

*World Email Directory*
http://www.worldemail.com
This site is dedicated to email, email, more email, finding people and locating businesses and organisations. WED has access to an estimated 18 million email addresses and more than 140 million business and phone addresses world wide. You will find everything from email software, to email list servers, golobal email databases, business, telephone and fax directories and a powerful email search engine.

*Yahoo!*
http://www.yahoo.com
http://www.yahoo.co.uk
Yahoo! was the first substantial internet directory, and continues to be one of the best for free general searching. It contains over a billion links categorised by subject. You can 'drill down' through the well-organised categories to find what you want, or you can carry out your own searches using keywords. The site also offers world news, sport, weather, email, chat, retailing facilities, clubs and many other features. Yahoo! is probably one of the search engines and directories you will use time after time, as do millions of people every day. Look for the link to Busi-

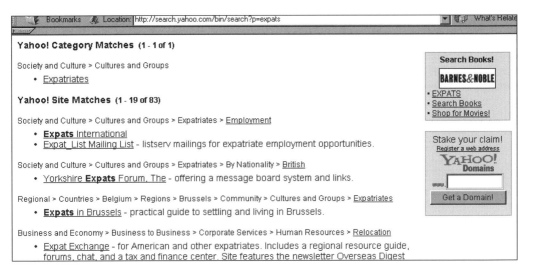

ness and Economy. From there you can click on Employment for thousands of links.

## Search utilities

*WebFerret*
http://www.ferretsoft.com
WebFerret is an excellent search utility. You can key in your query offline, and when you connect it searches the web until it has collected all the references you have specified – up to 9,999 if you wish. WebFerret queries ten or more search engines simultaneously and discards any

Fig. 21. Yahoo! is one of the best known and most visited search engines on the internet.

Fig. 22. Using the utility Webferret to search for expat information.

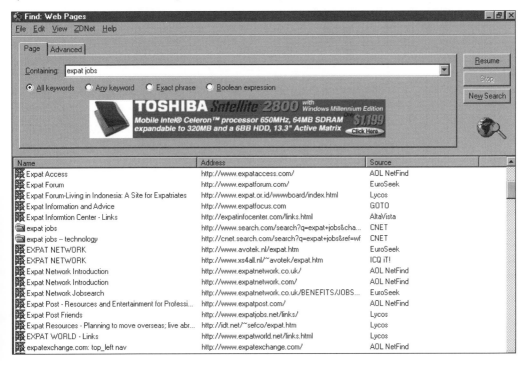

duplicate results. The search engines it queries include AltaVista, Yahoo!, Infoseek, Excite, and various others. You can immediately visit the web pages it lists for you, even while WebFerret is still running. The trial version of the program is free, and simplicity itself. It only takes a few minutes to download from FerretSoft. Highly recommended.

## Newsgroups and internet mailing lists

▶ *Newsgroups* – are public discussion groups freely available on the internet. Each newsgroup is a collection of messages, usually unedited and not checked by anyone ('unmoderated'). Messages can be posted in the newsgroup, and read, by anyone including you. The ever-growing newsgroups have been around for much longer than the world wide web and web pages, and are an endless source of information, news, scandal, entertainment, resources and ideas. The 80,000-plus newsgroups are collectively referred to as Usenet. To access newsgroups, you will need a news reader, a type of software that enables you to search, read, post and manage messages in a newsgroup. It will normally be supplied as part of your internet service when you first sign up, e.g. Internet Explorer/Outlook, or Netscape/Messenger.

Fig. 23. Reading a message posted in a newsgroup called 'alt.jobs.overseas'.

*news:alt.jobs.overseas*
*news:us.jobs.offered*
These are just two just examples of Usenet newsgroups. To access any such group, just type the address exactly as shown above into your

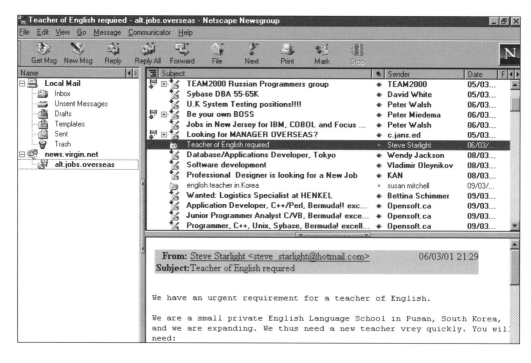

browser's address box: the name of the newsgroup, prefixed (as in the two headings show above) by:

news:

After a few seconds, your computer's newsreader will open up (probably Outlook, or Netscape Messenger) and the messages in the newsgroup should open up for you automatically. Click on any of the headers (single-line descriptions) in the upper panel, and you can then read the message in the lower panel.

*Deja.com*
http://www.deja.com
Deja.com (originally Deja News) was founded in 1995 as the first web site dedicated exclusively to online discussion, and capable of searching and archiving Usenet newsgroups. With more than six million page views per day, it offers access to more than 45,000 newsgroups. Deja is one of the web's most visited sites. More than a million people have registered (free) to take advantage of its expanding range of information and community services. It has recently been acquired by Google, with a new address:

http://groups.google.com

▶ *Mailing lists* – In internet parlance, a mailing list is a forum where members can distribute messages by email to the members of the forum, and where all the members ('subscribers') can read the messages posted. There are two types of lists, discussion and announcement. Discussion lists allow exchange between list members. Announcement lists are one-way only and used to distribute information such as news or humour. The best place to look for specific mailing lists is Liszt (see below).

*Liszt*
http://www.liszt.com
Liszt offers the largest index of mailing lists available on the internet, covering every conceivable area of interest – more than 90,000 lists in all. It also offers a Usenet newsgroups directory and an IRC chat directory. You can obtain a great deal of information here.

*MailBase*
http://www.mailbase.ac.uk
Run from the University of Sheffield, MailBase is the best-known and largest source of special interest mailing lists in the UK, over 2,000 in all. You can search its database of lists to find the one(s) that interest you, and then subscribe (free) to read and post messages on that particular topic – politics, business topics, health, or what you will.

# Searching for information.........................................

### More Internet Handbooks to help you

*Discussion Forums on the Internet*, Kye Valongo. All about newsgroups and mailing lists.

*Finding a Job on the Internet*, Brendan Murphy (2nd edition).

*Exploring Yahoo! on the Internet*, David Holland. Using Yahoo! for searches, email, chat and more.

*Getting Started on the Internet*, Kye Valongo. A guide for absolute beginners.

*Search Engines on the Internet*, Kye Valongo. All about search engines and how to use them.

*Where to Find It on the Internet*, Kye Valongo (2nd edition).

# 6 Expat web sites

**In this chapter we will explore:**

▶ *portal sites for expats*
▶ *portal sites for newspapers and magazines*
▶ *publications for expats*
▶ *general interest*

. . . . . . . . . . . . . . . . . . . . . . . . . . . . . . . . . . . . . . . . . . . . .

## Portal sites for expats

*Amazon.co.uk*
http://www.amazon.co.uk
Amazon offers a comprehensive list of working overseas research reference books, travel guides, and indeed millions of books on every subject under the sun.

*American Foreign Service Families*
http://www.aafsw.org
Intended primarily for American State department families, it is worth checking out for its content and links. Livelines, its internet discussion group, brings the foreign service community together to exchange information and engage in lively debates on topical issues.

*Australians Abroad*
http://www.australiansabroad.com
Australians Abroad was founded in 1996 to provide a centralised resource for Australians living overseas. All the work for Australians Abroad is on a volunteer and unpaid basis.

*Back To My Roots*
http://www.backtomyroots.com
This is a new global community for expatriates and exchange students. In this community, you will find interesting information about both your home country and the country in which you are (temporarily) residing.

*British Council*
http://www.britcoun.org
The aim of the Council is to create enduring partnerships between British and other cultures by creating opportunities to connect with the latest skills, ideas and experience from the UK. You can visit their offices in 243 towns and cities in 110 countries or contact their specialist teams from anywhere on this site to find out what they can do for you.

*British Expats*
http://britishexpats.com/
This excellent developing site is described as 'a resource and hangout for British expats around the world.' Features include current news from the

**BritishExpats**
*serving the expat community*

| Home | Links | Add

Welcome to the British expats link archive. A
 you own or know of a site that caters for

**Categories:**
**Employment** (12)
New Zealand, USA, United Kingdom ...

**Family and Lifestyle** (20)
Education, Health, Relocation ...

**Finance** (5)
Credit, Investments, Mortgages ...

**Housing** (6)
Europe, Far East
There are 150 links for you to ch

# Expat web sites ............................................

UK, US immigration specific news, contributed articles from anyone who wants to make themselves heard, in-depth immigration information, online discussion, and expat related links.

*Canadian Foreign Service Families*
http://www.fsca-acse.org
This site is run by the Foreign Service Community Association for Canadian diplomatic families. It contains lots of links and helpful information.

*Directories: Worldwide & Other Countries*
http://www.dis.strath.ac.uk/business/directories.html
Maintained at the University of Strathclyde, this page has links to worldwide directories and directories covering specific countries and regions. Recommended as a basic resource.

*Economist Intelligence Unit*
http://www.eiu.com
The EIU produces objective and timely analysis and forecasts of the political, economic and business environment in more than 180 countries. It also produces reports on certain strategic industries and on the latest management thinking.

*EMDS*
http://www.emdsnet.com/index.shtml
Here you will find a company which organises a number of job fairs each year e.g. Euro Managers, Asia Managers Forum, Africa Managers Forum as well as more general international recruitment work.

*Employment Index*
http://www.employmentindex.com
This is a useful portal site with four main sections on the home page. You can link into employment, job seekers links worldwide, and search engines.

*Escape Artist*
http://www.escapeartist.com/
Here is an ultimate internet resource for careers overseas, especially if you would like to go offshore and escape the relentless rise of taxation. This is a web site for anyone moving to another country, expatriates, overseas job seekers, tax exiles, adventurers and freedom seekers everywhere. There are well-categorised links to all kinds of useful information, for example the world's top newspapers, a world reference desk, an expatriate's book store, the world's search engines, Latin-American search engines, a countries index and stuff on global human freedom. It can help you build up your own internet commerce, with help on telecommuting, web communications, net office and web phones for expats. Find out about global investments, tax havens, stock markets of the world, offshore credit cards, offshore real estate and offshore banks. There are links to jobs overseas, embassy pages, moving overseas, and international living magazine – in fact just about every-

Fig. 24. Escape Artist is one of the essential internet bookmarks for the serious expat wanting to maximise their overseas experience.

thing you need to succeed as an internationally mobile and potentially tax-free professional anywhere on the planet.

## Expat Access

http://www.expataccess.com

Based in Belgium, this is a useful site for expats living in Europe. Using the power of the internet, it provides information and creates connections between individual expatriates, personnel departments responsible for expatriation, and companies providing products and services to these groups.

## Expat Exchange

http://www.expatexchange.com

Founded in 1997, Expat Exchange has become one of the largest online communities for English-speaking expatriates. Consisting of over 140 country and topic networks that can be accessed by free subscription, the community says it has supported over 400,000 expats. Recommended.

## Expat Forum

http://www.expatforum.com

Expat Forum is an American-based source of information, services and chat about living, working, travelling, and doing business overseas. Its bookstore selections offer choices for the best practical guides for living overseas. It does not run a jobs database. The site is a project of HR International, an independent human resources consulting firm based in Maryland.

# Expat web sites ...........................................................

*Expat Moms*
http://www.expat-moms.com
This site has been put together by a British mother who wants to share information and ideas about parenting.

*Expat Network*
http://www.expatnetwork.co.uk
Expat Network will help you find a job overseas and will provide assistance once you are working. Established in 1989, it has obtained overseas employment for over 9,000 people using its vast pool of resources and contacts. It publishes a monthly magazine, *Nexus*, which is more than just a job supplement. It is also packed with interesting and informative articles written specifically for people who want to or who already work abroad. The job search section of the magazine consists of around 12 pages packed full of jobs, of which a representative selection is shown on this site. Expat Network is one of the essential UK contact points for people considering an international career move. The company is based in Croydon, Surrey.

Fig. 25. Expat Network is a popular and well-established UK-based service.

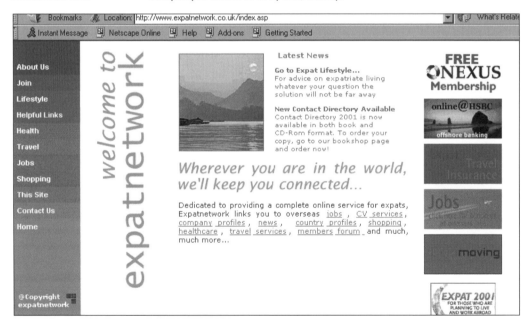

*Expat Spouse*
http://www.expatspouse.com
This site offers an advice service for expatriates working abroad and their families, with information about relocation and the practical problems associated with settling down in foreign climes. Those who have taken the plunge can discuss their experiences at the Expat Cafe chat forum.

*Expat Village*
http://www.expatvillage.com
This is a South American web site run from Buenos Aires, Argentina. It provides advice and information about international relocation, dining,

culture, tourism, shopping, community, parenting, city living and working abroad.

*Expatriates.com*
http://www.expatriates.com
The Paris-based site features a bulletin board for classified ads, a discussion board for direct communication with other expatriates, a resource directory of about 400 expatriate-related web sites, and selected articles by journalists and expatriates.

*Expatriate Living*
http://www.suite101.com/welcome.cfm/expatriate_living
Journalist Huw Francis has assembled lots of articles, links, and chat groups to help expats adjust to life abroad.

*Expatriate Clubs*
http://dir.clubs.yahoo.com/cultures___community/groups/expatriates/
This is a directory of more than 130 expatriate clubs at Yahoo!. Despite the long address, it is well worth exploring as a lively source of messages and news from expats the world over.

*Foreign and Commonwealth Office*
http://www.fco.gov.uk
This is an official UK government site with essential information about travel, visas, and the world's troublespots.

*Going Global*
http://www.goingglobal.de
Going Global is an online service for German speaking expatriates. With an emphasis on information, networking and individual counselling, it supports expat families during all stages of an international assignment.

*How to Get an Overseas Job*
http://homepages.tesco.net/ ~ Ken.Creffield/
Fancy a change of career and country? Written by an executive of the UK job hunters' newspaper *Overseas Jobs Express*, this site is packed with links to the job advertisement pages of organisations and newspapers abroad.

*iAgora*
http://www.iagora
This is a portal for those travelling, studying and working abroad. It includes some forums for the exchange of ideas and views, travel guides and the latest news and views from countries across the globe. On the following page you can search for your ideal internship in a specific country or by choosing the field in which you'd like to do an internship on this site.

http://www.iagora.com/iwork/jobdatabase/internships.html

**expatriates.com**
the online
community
for expatriates

Home Page

Classifieds

Resource Directory

Discussion Board

Subscribe

Unsubscribe

# Expat web sites .....................................................

*InfoSpace*
http://www.infospace.com/info/index_int.htm
From here you can explore yellow pages and white pages for the USA, Canada, UK, Germany, Belgium, Luxembourg, Italy, Spain and Austria. It includes a directory of email addresses. Data sources include InfoUSA, Acxiom (Canada), 192.com (UK), and Kapitol (for other European countries). You can also select many other countries from a box at the top of the page, and this gives a page including a link to a yellow pages service for that country, as well as the relevant section in the Open Directory.

*Monster Research Companies*
http://www.changejobs.co.uk/f_grad_3_m.html
The site will link you directly to loads of companies listed in alphabetical order.

*Outpost Expat*
http://www.outpostexpat.nl
Developed by Shell, this is a very thorough and well-organised collection of practical country information and links created to help expatriate families on the move.

*Pay Away*
http://www.payaway.co.uk
Fed up with the rat race? Got a year out and don't know what to do with it? This site supplies a wide range of job suggestions around the world and tells you where to look and who to approach to do something about it.

*Riley Guide*
http://www.dbm.com/jobguide/
This well-established employment portal site is dedicated to employment opportunities and job resources on the internet. You can access a comprehensive and businesslike set of links covering everything from preparing for a job search, resumes and cover letters, to targeting and researching employers, executing your job search campaign, job listings, networking, interviewing, negotiating, salary guides and guidance. There are lists of top companies, professional bodies and many useful worldwide links.

*Telephone Directories on the Web*
http://www.teldir.com/eng/
This is one of the internet's most complete index of online phone books, with over 400 links to yellow pages, white pages, business directories, email addresses and fax listings from over 170 countries all around the world. An essential reference for expats.

*Working Abroad*
http://www.fedora.csu.ac.uk/student/cidd/specials/abroad/Adds.htm#icd
You can link here to loads of addresses and web sites for working abroad.

*Working Abroad from the UK*
http://www.namss.org.uk/jobsaway.htm
Here you can find links to useful sites for working abroad. The site is maintained by the UK National Association of Managers of Student Services.

*Working in Different Countries*
http://www.fedora.csu.ac.uk/student/cidd/specials/abroad/CbyC.htm
Explore working in a number of different countries.

*Yahoo! Countries*
http://www.yahoo.co.uk/regional/countries/
Each country has a section on business and economy where you can find trade links, business opportunities, economic links, tax information, company listings and much more. This site makes a great starting point for your research.

*Yahoo! Embassies and Consulates*
http://uk.dir.yahoo.com/government/Embassies_and_Consulates/

## Portal sites for newspapers and magazines

▶ *Tip* – Newspapers and magazines are an important survival tool for prospective and actual expats. They can be a valuable source of local and company news, economic trends, and of current job vacancies. The internet now makes it possible to explore news media all over the world from the comfort of your own desktop.

*AJR NewsLink*
http://www.newslink.org/news.html
The site provides lots of links to online newspapers around the world.

*All Newspapers*
http://www.allnewspapers.com
Offers links to top stories and to local, national, and international newspapers, magazines, electronic media, and news agencies.

*Alternative Press Index*
http://www.altpress.org
Founded in 1969, the API is one of the oldest self-sustaining alternative media institutions in the United States. It has been recognized as a leading guide to the alternative press in the USA and around the world. Its well-organised online directory includes publications currently indexed in its own database and members of the Independent Press Association. Subscription information, email addresses and links to home pages are included. You can browse by title and by subject

*E&P Directory of Online Newspapers*
http://www.mediainfo.com/emedia/
This is a substantial database of newspapers and radio stations from all over the world. It includes a range of clearly set out search functions

and listings to get you started. The database contains over 12,000 records – well worth checking out.

*Ecola's Newsstand Directory*
http://www.ecola.com/news/press/
Logically organized links provide easy access to periodicals worldwide. Over 8,400 newspapers and magazines are listed, all of which are maintained by a paper-printed publication, and which provide English language content online. Recommended.

*Electronic Newsstand*
http://www.image.dk/~knud-sor/en/
This enterprising resource contains links to a vast number and variety of international news sources, supported by quick reference regional maps. Definitely worth exploring.

*MetaGrid Newspapers & Magazines*
http://www.metagrid.com/
The site enables you to search for both magazines and newspapers. Magazines are categorised by subject matter, and newspapers by continent and country.

*Mountain Breeze US and International Newspapers*
http://www.mountain-breeze.com/newspapers/index.html
Here you can visit a wide range of online international newspapers.

*News Central*
http://www.all-links.com/newscentral/
More than 3,500 newspaper links are currently available here.

*News Directory*
http://www.newsdirectory.com/
The site contains over 17,000 categorised information links.

*Newslink*
http://ajr.newslink.org/news.html
Here, you can find listings of papers for the USA and the rest of the world.

*Online Newspapers*
http://www.webwombat.coman/intercom/newsprs/index.htm
This site lists over 1400 newspapers from around the world by country and alphabetically. The links are active and take you straight into the newspapers' home pages. Not all of them have job ads but many do. This is an excellent resource for locating both national and local newspapers around the world. Especially useful for those wanting to work abroad, with a particular country in mind.

*PubList*
http://www.publist.com

PUB LIST

Free PubList.com Newsletter

Enter Email

Sign Up

**Publishers feature your publications!**

PubList.com is a massive internet-based reference for over 150,000 domestic and international print and electronic publications. These include magazines, journals, e-journals, newsletters, and monographs. It provides quick and easy access to detailed publication information including, titles, formats, publisher addresses, editor contacts, circulation data, and ISSN numbers. The site also provides access to subscription services as well as article level information through rights and permissions providers and document delivery services.

## Publications for expats

*Exact*
http://www.cant.ac.uk/exact/linkrefs/refs/keynotes.htm
This explains a leaflet containing careers information for adults planning to work abroad. See also:

http://www.cant.ac.uk/exact/linkrefs/refs/scils.htm

This page contains information about leaflets dealing with voluntary work overseas, working abroad and working holidays.

*Information Sources*
http://www.fedora.csu.ac.uk/student/cidd/specials/abroad/Pubs.htm
Check this official UK Careers Services web site for some directories and books related to working abroad.

*Intercultural Press*
http://www.interculturalpress.com/
Intercultural Press is an established US publisher of practical books and materials in the field of intercultural relations.

*Nexus*
http://www.expatnetwork.co.uk/
This is a well-known UK-based monthly illustrated magazine for expatriates. See Expat Network above.

*Offshore Entrepreneur*
http://www.cyberhaven.com/offshore/
Making Money Offshore is a book by Adam Starchild offering a number of different roads to the creation and protection of wealth in foreign countries.

*Outbound Newspapers*
http://www.outbound-newspapers.com
Based in Eastbourne, UK, Outbound Newspapers publishes some excellent monthly newspapers for Australia, Canada, New Zealand, South Africa, and the USA. The newspapers are packed with helpful articles and features, display and classified advertising including for jobs, and guidance on obtaining passports, visas and work permits. Recommended.

# Expat web sites ...................................................

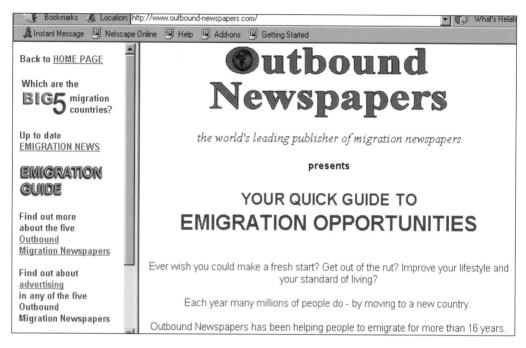

Back to HOME PAGE

Which are the

**BIG5** migration countries?

Up to date
EMIGRATION NEWS

**EMIGRATION GUIDE**

Find out more
about the five
Outbound
Migration Newspapers

Find out about
advertising
in any of the five
Outbound
Migration Newspapers

# ⊕utbound Newspapers

*the world's leading publisher of migration newspapers*

**presents**

## YOUR QUICK GUIDE TO
## EMIGRATION OPPORTUNITIES

Ever wish you could make a fresh start? Get out of the rut? Improve your lifestyle and your standard of living?

Each year many millions of people do - by moving to a new country.

Outbound Newspapers has been helping people to emigrate for more than 16 years.

Fig. 26. Outbound Newspapers publishes a range of newspapers with jobs and other features for expats.

*Overseas Jobs (About.com)*
http://www.overseasjobs.com/
This US-based web site offers a database of international vacancies for professionals, expatriates and adventure-seekers, with links to several associated web sites such as SummerJobs.com, AboutJobs.com, ResortJobs.com, and InternJobs.com.

*Overseas Jobs Express*
http://www.overseasjobsexpress.co.uk
The fortnightly Sussex-based newspaper *Overseas Job Express* currently contains about job 3,000 listings and other useful job information. On its web site you can search its growing database of vacancies by key-word, or browse it by job type. An outstanding feature of the site is its guide to over 700 career, employment, job and recruiter sites in 42 coun-tries. You can access these by clicking Africa, Asia, Australasia, Western Europe, Scandinavia, Eastern Europe, Russia, immigration, Middle East, USA, Mexico, Canada, South America, UK and international. Advertisers are invited to reach over 100,000 overseas job seekers each month by posting their international job listings on the site. If you have any intention of working overseas, this site is a must.

*Transitions Abroad Online*
http://www.transitionsabroad.com
Transitions Abroad is a bimonthly guide to practical information on affordable alternatives to mass tourism: living, working, studying, or vacationing alongside the people of the host country. The site also offers online articles and resources.

Fig. 27. Overseas Jobs Express is the UK's best known newspaper for international jobhunters.

*FT Expat*
http://www.ftexpat.com
New from the *Financial Times* and its sister magazine publication *Resident Abroad*, this is an authoritative site for expats, focussing on financial and lifestyle topics.

*International Living Magazine*
http://www.internationalliving.com
This is a monthly online newsletter on the subject, which also publishes a free weekly email newsletter. Its editors, contributors, and correspondents worldwide report on opportunities for travel, living, and investment.

*Journeywoman*
http://www.journeywoman.com
Here is an online travel resource just for women, full of practical information and fun.

*Weekly Telegraph*
http://www.globalnetwork.co.uk
Check out the online weekly version of this British daily newspaper for its Expat Living section. It covers personal finance and healthcare issues, property and education from an expat perspective.

*Woman Abroad Magazine*
http://www.womanabroad.com
This a new glossy publication for women on the move. This site will give

you an idea of what's in the latest magazine and does offer some stuff for free. Log on is required.

*Xpat*
http://www.xpat.nl
This site contains a large amount of basic information that will help make the Netherlands understandable. It is a site with many points of interest which will make your stay behind the dykes and the dunes an enjoyable one and will help you find your way through the jungle of written and unwritten rules, customs, habits and traditions.

## General interest

*True Globehopper?*
http://www.labourmobility.com/trueglobehopper.htm
Try this interactive test and check out the qualities you may need for working in management in another country.

*Usit Now*
http://www.usitnow.ie/countries/ireland/frames/fram_workabroad.htm
Usit Work Abroad Programmes allow you to gain an insight into the local way of life and can help get you there with discount flights, cheap air fares etc.

*Women Working Worldwide*
http://www.poptel.org.uk/women-ww/
Working Worldwide is a UK based organisation which supports women workers in the global economy through information exchange and international networking.

*Work Experience Bank*
http://www.workbank.man.ac.uk/
This is a resource for students, employers and academics. Using this site will give you access to information and work experience opportunities in the UK and overseas.

*Working Abroad Seminars*
http://www.bma.org.uk/wabroad.htm
Run by the British Medical Association, these seminars are open to doctors and medical students in the UK who are considering working (at postgraduate level) in another country but are not sure how to go about it.

# 7 Current expat vacancies

In this chapter we will explore:

▶ *international recruitment agencies*
▶ *job databases*

. . . . . . . . . . . . . . . . . . . . . . . . . . . . . . . . . . . . . . . . . . . . . . . . . . . . . . . . . . . . . . . . . . . . . . . . . . .

## International recruitment agencies

*Acumen*
http://www.acumen.demon.co.uk
Acumen is a contract and permanent personnel agency which provides staffing services to the pharmaceutical, biotech and healthcare industries throughout the UK. It provides personnel for engineering, technical, scientific and manufacturing environments. The site is directed mainly at client organisations. A useful feature of the site is its links to leading UK and international chemicals and pharmaceutical employers.

*Angel International Recruitment*
http://www.angel-int.co.uk
Angel promotes the placing of temporary staff within the commercial, medical, hotel catering and driving arenas. This site has a very straightforward feedback form that can be used to declare an interest in a particular service.

*Astbury Marsden*
http://astburymarsden.co.uk
Astbury Marsden is an established name in IT and financial recruitment. The company offers opportunities in six divisions: information technology, middle office banking, commerce and industry, corporate finance, equity research and international sectors. Each section is derived into current vacancies listed by job type and each job is explained in full.

*Douglas Llambias Associates*
http://www.llambias.co.uk
London-based DLA is a leading provider of financial, IT and other specialist recruitment services to accountancy and legal firms, industrial and commercial companies, management consultancies and banking and financial services organisations, both nationally and internationally. The site contained several hundred vacancies, presented under broad industry categories, with brief details of each including remuneration levels, and online application forms.

*Hamilton Recruitment*
http://www.hamilton-recruitment.com
Hamilton recruits chartered accountants from the UK and North America to work in the world's premier financial centres such as Bermuda, the Caribbean and the Channel Islands. Here is your chance to earn a tax-free salary and enjoy an outstanding quality of life in these exciting international locations.

# Current expat vacancies ........................................

Fig. 28. International Recruitment Consultants.

*International Recruitment Consultants*
http://www.international-recruitment.co.uk
See these web pages for overseas jobs with immediate and permanent careers. There are opportunities for business executives, hotel managers, catering managers, special event organisers, directors, accountants, senior management personnnel, high profile secretaries, senior administration staff, architects, financiers, IT administrators, computer programmers, analysts, and networking consultants.

*Manpower*
http://www.manpower.com
Established in 1948, Manpower is the largest staffing and employment service in the world. With more than 3,000 offices in 50 countries, it has provided employment opportunities for millions of people. On its international web site you can use the various clickable colour maps to find its offices in almost every part of the world.

*Network Overseas*
http://www.networkoverseas.cc
This company recruits qualified professionals in engineering and construction, information technology, teaching, medical, nursing and ancillary hospital services for clients across the world, with special emphasis on the Middle East.

*Price Jamieson*
http://www.pricejam.com
UK and international media, marketing and communications vacancies are listed on this site.

*Robert Half & Accountemps*
http://195.99.180.2/job.html
Robert Half & Accountemps is the largest and longest established (1948) specialist in accountancy and finance recruitment, with 225 offices worldwide. Established in the UK in 1973, it now has 17 regional offices. The company has a global turnover in excess of $1.3 billion. 'Our business is to help people like you gain an edge in the recruitment marketplace whether you're looking for a permanent or temporary position, or just like to keep your options open.'

## Job databases

*80 Days*
http://www.overseasjobs.co.uk
Come to this site to find mega job sites in the USA, Australia, Europe and the rest of the world.

*BioMedNet Jobs*
http://biomednet.com/jobs.htm
This is a London-based worldwide club for the biological and medical community, now part of Reed plc. Its Job Exchange contains nearly 1,000 positions wanted and available in academia and commercial sectors. You can search the jobs database, add your own job advertisement or CV, check out many links to career sites, books and articles, and access other resources to help your job search. You have to complete quite a detailed online application form to register. The site is believed to have in excess of 400,000 subscribers.

*Bioscience Jobs*
http://www.bioscience-jobs.com
This is an online UK-based confidential CV database for life science graduates. It specialises in employment opportunities in the biomolecular sciences. It welcomes submission of CVs, enquiries about specific posts and requests to advertise job opportunities or search its database of potential candidates. It especially welcomes skills in bioinformatics, 3d structure determination, molecular modelling, protein and peptide chemistry, structural and functional genomics, molecular immunology, and computational chemistry. Job seekers are invited to complete the online form to provide basic details of their qualifications and current experience. The service is mainly seeking candidates with postgraduate experience in industry or basic research.

*Datum Online*
http://www.datumeurope.com
'The ultimate job site on the internet' – connects you to big firms advertising their vacancies in the UK, the rest of Europe, USA and the Asia/

# Current expat vacancies ..............................................

Pacific rim. There are site links to jobs by email, an IT jobs section, create your résumé, career advice, and graduates. Free registration is required.

*Expat Jobs Net*
http://expat.ft.com/expat
They say: 'There are now over 50,000 vacancies in the master database.' The site also has a useful collection of links for expat living.

*Hotrecruit*
http://www.hotrecruit.co.uk
The site, which launched in 2000, says it is the first recruitment site in the UK to cater specifically for students and antipodeans. It offers jobs from all skilled and unskilled sectors including media and new media, teaching and childcare, medical and healthcare, telecoms and call centres, hospitality retail, fast food, travel and leisure, insurance and legal, sales and marketing, crazy jobs, accountancy and finance, IT, secretarial and admin, and construction and trades. Its 'crazy jobs' section is for those

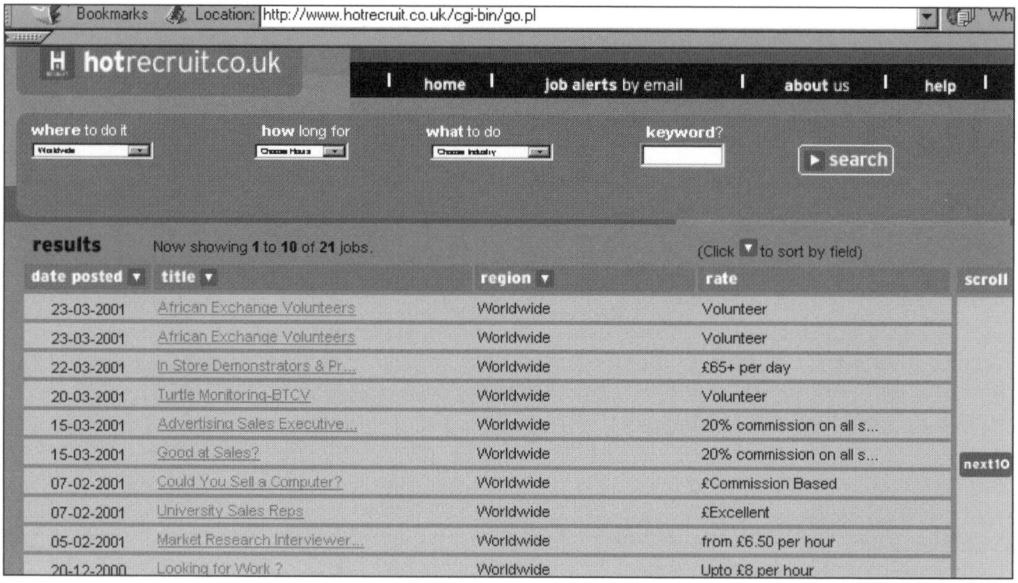

Fig. 29. Hot Recruit runs a very lively site for job hunters.

who want to escape the routine of nine to five, offering a wide range of weird and wonderful positions – many not for the faint-hearted. For example: 'Rice paddies and rickshaws. Bar managers required in the jungles of Cambodia.' You can get job alerts by email.

*International Jobs Magazine*
http://www.expat-magazine.com
If you can read French, this site is a must, packed with opportunities and country information.

*Monster*
http://www.monster.co.uk
This is a substantial vacancies database, and part of the global Monster jobs network. When reviewed it contained around 11,000 UK jobs,

26,000 European jobs, and 440,000 global jobs. Features of the site include: My Monster, CV management, a personal job search agent, a careers network, message boards, privacy options, expert advice on job-seeking and career management and free newsletters.

*NetJobs*
http://www.netjobs.co.uk
This is a big site with a directory made up of about 100 online recruitment agencies and a searchable index of permanent and contract jobs, mostly IT-related.

*Overseas Jobs*
http://www.overseasjobs.com
The site offers a broad coverage of international jobs, careers and work abroad. You will find thousands of detailed listings for paid internships, seasonal work, volunteer opportunities, overseas jobs, and many others.
*People Bank*

Fig. 30. The web site of a popular US-based service, Overseas Jobs. There are links from here to SummerJobs.com, AboutJobs.com, ResortJobs.com and InternJobs.com.

http://www.peoplebank.com
This well-established service uses the internet to match employers and employees. It has a database of over 100,000 registered candidates, for whom the service is free.

*Prospects International Job Links*
http://www.prospects.csu.ac.uk/emp/
This is part of Prospects, the UK's official graduate careers service. Look for the Useful Links section, where you will find a whole array of international jobs links for Europe and the rest of the world.

# Current expat vacancies .............................................

*StepStone*
http://www.stepstone.co.uk
Launched in 1996, and with offices in London, StepStone has rapidly grown into one of Europe's leading online recruiting companies, offering one of the largest employment databases on the internet. It offers around 115,000 job vacancies and attracts around 3 million user sessions to the its web sites every month. It has over 420,000 registered subscribers and is used by more than 12,000 companies across Europe. You can search a wide range of occupational categories.

*The Job*
http://www.thejob.com
Thousands of jobs across the UK and Europe are listed in this site. So whether you're experienced, or a graduate searching for your first placement, you should be able to find what you're looking for.

*Top Jobs on the Net*
http://www.topjobs.net/
Visit this site for UK and international jobs (currently Australia, Ireland, Netherlands, Norway, Poland, Sweden, Thailand, and UK). You can search by job category. Visit articles and advice, online career influences and career expectations surveys (from ASE), CV preparation checklists, opportunities, preparing for interviews & assessments and links to ASE psychometric assessment guides.

Fig. 31.
Top Jobs on the Net is one of the better known sites for overseas job hunters.

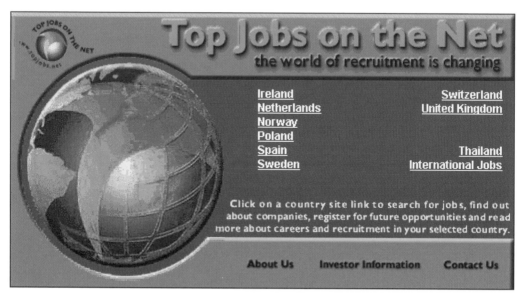

*Top Jobs on the Net International*
http://www.topjobs.co.uk/
This page profiles those companies who are recruiting worldwide for mobile, world-class professionals with more jobs in country-specific databases. See also:

http://www.international.topjobs.net/

*World Careers Network*

http://www.wcn.co.uk

'Matching students and firms worldwide', this site contains detailed information on a large number of recruiters and job vacancies. You can access a contact database of more than 10,000 employers worldwide, read news, and explore links to recruiters on the net. You can also upload your CV for recruiters to access. However, to use the site you first have to agree to its lengthy list of conditions and obtain a personal user name and password. The site restricts access to currently enrolled students. It verifies that you are currently affiliated as a student by checking your email address against a database of email patterns. The site can be read in German as well as English.

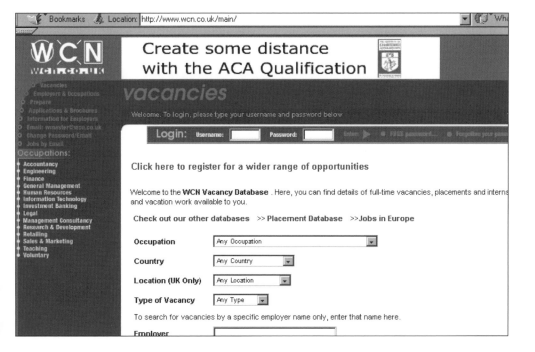

# 8 Country information

**In this chapter we will explore:**

▶ *Africa*
▶ *Australia and New Zealand*
▶ *Europe*
▶ *The Far East*
▶ *The Middle East*
▶ *The United States and Canada*
▶ *South America and the Caribbean*

. . . . . . . . . . . . . . . . . . . . . . . . . . . . . . . . . . . . . . . . . . . . . . . . . . . . . . . . . . . . . . . . . . . . .

## Africa

*African Management Services Company*
http://www.amsco.org
AMSCO is a United Nations project to make expatriate managers and funded training available to African companies.

*Africa Jobs & Employment Index*
http://www.escapeartist.com/jobs8/africa.htm
This is a useful expatriate resource, which forms part of the big Escape Artist web site.

*Computer Week Jobs Online (South Africa)*
http://www.jobs.co.za
This is a leading South African IT user publication. You can enter your CV into the database free of charge. To ensure confidentiality, only subscribing agencies have access to this database. You can search the job database free of charge. You can also access free online agency and employer directories containing corporate profiles of all corporate subscribers to the service.

*Personnel Net*
http://www.pnet.co.za
The site describes itself as the largest recruitment site in South Africa. You will typically find around 6,000 current vacancies. The site includes handy links to about 140 local recruitment agencies.

*South Africa: Braby's Directory*
http://www.brabys.co.za
Here you can explore a searchable database of contact details of 500,000 businesses across southern Africa.

## Australia and New Zealand

*Bryon Employment*
http://www.bryon.com.au
Byron Employment Australia was one of the first internet employment

sites in Australia. It operates primarily as a job-listing service, and does not provide services to individual candidates or accept résumés at present. However, it offers a huge selection of jobs around Australia, posted by advertising agencies, consultants, accountants and others. You can view its extensive agency directory on screen. The job are sorted under accounting, banking and finance, communications, construction, engineering, government, health care, human resources, hospitality, industrial, computers and IT, legal, management, sales and marketing, schools and colleges, science and technology, support staff, and tertiary. It has introduced a free set-and-forget email service, which automatically emails you details of those jobs on the database that match your search criteria. You can register your details using a simple form. Byron also includes links to other Australian employment-related resources, and includes valuable information for overseas candidates.

*Employment Australia*
http://www.employment.com.au
Enter this site for work opportunities in Australia. Established in Sydney in 1995, its 1,300-strong client base includes major corporations, management consultants, government statutory authorities and universities, Australia-wide.

Fig. 32. Employment.com of Australia is a must if you are serious about working down under.

*Interquest Australia*
http://www.jobserve.com/interquest/
InterQuest was formed in Australia in 1987 by IT executives who were specialists in their fields. Today it has over 400 contractors working worldwide. With an office in Highgate, London, the company acts as a conduit for Britons who want to work in Australia, and for Australians who come over to work in the UK.

*Job Net*

http://www.jobnet.com.au

Job Net offers the largest central index of computer, technology and management contract and permanent employment opportunities in Australia, New Zealand and Asia available through leading IT recruitment agencies. You can browse all the current job positions (updated daily) including skills specification and all contact details, or keyword search using the online database search facility. The current database is said to hold over 11,000 job positions. You can also join its free daily email alert service of new jobs which are delivered to you via email.

*Job Net*

http://www.jobnetnz.co.nz

This is a link to jobs primarily in New Zealand. You can search the local newspapers for appointments, or the New Zealand *InfoTech Weekly*. You can select the type of appointment, the newspaper source, region and town. When we checked, there were more than 800 vacancies on the database, the vast majority in *InfoTech Weekly*. The more general local newspapers database seemed to have very few.

*Jobz (Australia)*

http://jobz.ozware.com/

Jobz is a database of employment opportunities in Australia. Jobs are organised into numerous categories, with a link for each to aid your surfing. There may be less information than expected. Our test search for jobs in computing yielded only five results. Job descriptions were fairly brief.

*Monster Board (Australia)*

http://www.nj.com.au/

If you are hoping to live and work in Australia, this is a site you should visit, a Monster Board service geared to life down under. For job seekers there is a job search facility with hundreds of jobs to choose from, a personal job search agent to assist you, employer profiles, and a résumé builder.

*New Zealand Immigration Service*

http://www.immigration.govt.nz/

As official sites go, this is quite user-friendly. Some 250,000 visitors apparently accessed the site in the last year. You can check out migration requirements, the all important pass mark system, family categories, investor schemes, residency and citizenship, fees and forms, information for student visitors, FAQs, and more. You can download a whole series of informative booklets giving detailed information about living and working in New Zealand. If you feel serious about going, whether on a temporary or permanent basis, this site is a must.

*Working in Australia*

http://www.immi.gov.au/

This is an official site giving information about migration to Australia,

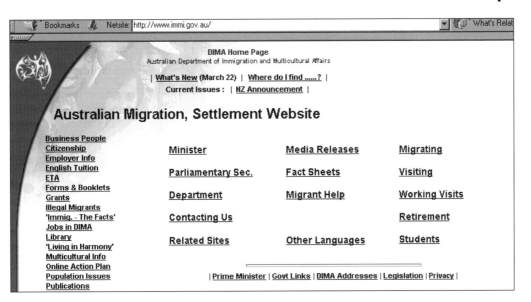

**DIMA Home Page**
Australian Department of Immigration and Multicultural Affairs

| **What's New** (March 22) | **Where do I find ......?** |
Current Issues : | **NZ Announcement** |

## Australian Migration, Settlement Website

**Business People**
**Citizenship**
**Employer Info**
**English Tuition**
**ETA**
**Forms & Booklets**
**Grants**
**Illegal Migrants**
**'Immig. - The Facts'**
**Jobs in DIMA**
**Library**
**'Living in Harmony'**
**Multicultural Info**
**Online Action Plan**
**Population Issues**
**Publications**

**Minister**     **Media Releases**     **Migrating**

**Parliamentary Sec.**     **Fact Sheets**     **Visiting**

**Department**     **Migrant Help**     **Working Visits**

**Contacting Us**     **Retirement**

**Related Sites**     **Other Languages**     **Students**

| **Prime Minister** | **Govt Links** | **DIMA Addresses** | **Legislation** | **Privacy** |

published by Australia's Department of Immigration and Multicultural Affairs. It gives a practical and thorough introduction to the immigration rules, visitors' permits, permanent and temporary residence, working visits, skilled migrants, studying in Australia, fact sheets, business immigration, the humanitarian program, retirement to Australia, Australian citizenship, government department links, and lots more. This site would be essential for anyone thinking of living or working in Australia whether short term or permanently.

Fig. 33. Working in Australia, the web site of the Australian Department of Immigration and Multicultural Affairs. It contains lots of practical pointers for people hoping to live and work in Australia.

## Europe

*Arbeitsamt (Germany)*
http://www.arbeitsamt.de
This is an official German employment information site. The pages are in German, and there is no English translation option. The site is efficiently organised into numerous regional categories and sub-categories, with clear clickable colour maps of regions and cities, to help you find your way around.

*Arbetsförmedlingen Internet (Sweden)*
http://www.umu.se/af
This large database of job vacancies in Sweden is maintained by the National Labour Market Board of Sweden. The site is updated daily, but you will need to be able to read some Swedish.

*Avotek Publishing (Netherlands)*
http://www.xs4all.nl/ ~ avotek
Thus Dutch-based publishing company offers several useful guides to the European job market including the Netherlands. The site includes information on the many head-hunter directories it publishes, plus links to international job banks, recruiters and other sources.

# Country information .................................................

### Belgium Career Web

http://belgium.careerweb.com

Yes! This site is in English. Looking for a professional, technical or managerial job? Here you'll find many listings for high-paying, interesting positions with companies that you want to work for. There are jobs in engineering, information systems, telecommunications, marketing, accounting, healthcare and many other fields. All the companies listed have profile pages with corporate, product and employee benefits information.

### Cadres Online (France)

http://www.cadresonline.com

Though slow-loading, this site looks to be a useful resource for French-speakers seeking work in France, complete with salary guides and other supportive information for applicants. You have to complete and submit an online CV, and will then be emailed details of vacancies matching your qualifications. It did not seem to be possible to do the usual kind of database job search. They say that about 3,700 vacancies had been notified by employers during the previous month. There was no English translation option on the site.

### Careercare

http://www.careercare.com

You can access permanent and contract IT work opportunities in Europe through this Edinburgh-based company.

### Career Net (Germany)

http://www.careernet.de

This is a German job service, Stellenangebote und Bewerbungen Online, now being developed by the ever-expanding StepStone organisation.

Fig. 34. If you are hoping to work in Germany, the Career Net web site is well worth a visit.

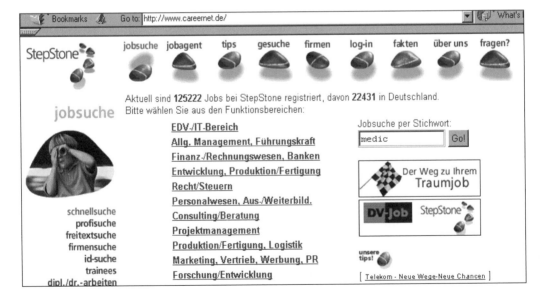

*Careers Europe*
http://www.careerseurope.co.uk
This Bradford-based service is part of the EU's Euroguidance network which exists to exchange careers information and good practice between the member states of the EU and EEA, in order to promote vocational mobility. The site outlines study, work and training opportunities across Europe, and includes some useful links.

*CAROL (Company Annual Reports Online)*
http://www.carol.co.uk
This is a free service offering online access to company reports for Europe, Asia and the USA.

*CICA (France)*
http://emploi.cica.fr
This is a French employment site offering some job and training information about the Provence-Alpes and Côte d'Azur regions. The site is naturally in French, and there is no option for English translation.

*Citizens First*
http://citizens.eu.int
Through this home page you can find key information on European countries including living, working, studying, training and doing research, buying goods and services, travelling, equal opportunities and looking for work.

*Creyf's (Belgium)*
http://www.creyfs.be
Creyf's recruits for temporary technical and engineering personnel in Belgium. Information on who they are and how to contact them is given in English, French, German and Dutch on this slow-loading site.

*Daley Recruitment (Belgium)*
http://www.rdas.co.uk/BelgiumJobs.htm
Contract and permanent job opportunities in Belgium can be found here.

*Danish Employment Service*
http://www.af.dk
You will need Danish to use this official Arbejdsformidlingen site, which contains in-depth information about job opportunities and vacancies in Denmark. It includes a job bank, CV bank service, and email updates.

*Eastern & Central European Job Bank*
http://www.ecejobbank.com
This is a free service, developed in Hungary by an IT company, to help companies and skilled workers find each other in the region. Job seekers can browse job listings, and post their résumés for employers to see. Employers can list their openings. When we checked, there were only 16 postings in the job bank, including several for financial personnel.

*Elstead Maps (Spain)*
http://www.elstead.co.uk/spawor.htm
The company offers a range of commercially published guides to living and working in Spain.

*EURES Services*
http://www.fas.ie/gairm/services/1_2.htm
EURES is a system for the exchange of information on employment opportunities in the European Economic Area. It can be used by people who travel to work within the following countries: Belgium, Denmark, France, Germany, Greece, Ireland, Italy, Luxembourg, Portugal, Spain, The Netherlands, The United Kingdom, Austria, Finland, Norway, Sweden and Iceland. EURES has a European wide network of over 450 specially trained placement officers who are capable of advising job seekers and employers on aspects of living and working conditions in the various states of the EURES system.

*EURES Employment Information*
http://europa.eu.int/comm/employment_social/info.html
You can link into a European labour market network which offers some useful information on finding a job in Europe, including tips on international CVs, self-employment, living and working conditions, social security and addresses of advisers. The site is offered in German, English and French.

*Eurograduate*
http://www.eurograduate.com
Check out this site for graduate careers, career planning and jobs database for European opportunities. You can search by industry, occupation, qualification, and country of employment. There are also useful sections on finding and applying for jobs and preparing CVs for individual countries in Scandinavia, western Europe, southern Europe, and central and eastern Europe.

Fig. 35. At the Eurograduate web site you can find expert advice on career planning, useful links to other great sites and various postgraduate options.

*Europages Business Directory*
http://www.europages.com
This directory offers 500,000 companies selected in 30 European countries. The site is available is several languages.

*Europages' Business Information*
http://www.europages.com/home-en.html
This is a well-established directory of basic details of 500,000 companies from 30 European countries, searchable by name or product. It also has: economic overviews, list of selected trade fairs, reports on business trends in Europe, articles on European business topics (e.g. the Euro), links to national statistics offices, list of European Chambers, links to European yellow pages directories. You can view the site in English, French, German, Italian, or Spanish.

*Europages Link Resources*
http://www.webpromotion.co.uk/resourcelinks.htm
Use this site to find complimentary companies to target for links. There is a nice ability to find online businesses sorted by sector.

*European Info Centres*
http://www.euro-info.org.uk
EICs provide local access to a range of specialist information and advisory services for companies which are developing their businesses in Europe.

*European Living Conditions Information Directory*
http://europa.eu.int/scadplus/citizens/en/inter.htm
Here you can find information on legal and political systems, culture/social life, salaries and taxation, health services and social welfare and education systems in the European Union member states.    ELCID

Fig. 36. European Living Conditions is an excellent practical resource to living and working in the various EU member states.

stands for the European Living Conditions Information Directory. The ELCID database will tell you where you can find information on topics as: legal and political systems, culture and social life, salaries and taxation, health services, social welfare and education systems in the EU member states. This database was made – and is regularly updated – by Expertise in Labour Mobility for the European Foundation in Dublin, Ireland.

### European Resources
http://www.e-r.co.uk
ER is a recruitment agency specialising in graduates and others with language skills. It specialises in multilingual call centre recruitment in the Netherlands and Germany.

### Expatica (Benelux)
http://www.expatica.com
This wide-ranging site (formerly Xpat.net) features local news and community listings for English-speaking expatriates in the Netherlands and has just expanded into Belgium.

### Expats in Brussels (Belgium)
http://www.expatsinbrussels.com
A professional looking resource, complete with numerous informative articles which can be read in several different languages.

### Harvey Nash
http://www.harveynash-contracts.com
European IT contract opportunities can be found here for Germany, Switzerland and the Benelux countries.

### IBNIX Recruitment
http://www.ibnix.co.uk
Visit this site for European contract vacancies. The firm has head offices in London and Sydney and regional branches located throughout UK, Europe and the Asia-Pacific region.

### Intermediair (Netherlands)
http://www.bpa.nl/intermediair
This is a comprehensive jobs and career site for the Netherlands, updated every Wednesday. It contains detailed information about salaries, careers, and recruitment, based on the weekly magazine of the same name. But you'll need to understand Dutch to use the site – there's no English translation. Intermediair is a project of VNU Business Publications.

### Irish Jobs Page
http://www.exp.ie
Operated from Dublin, the businesslike Irish Jobs Page claims to be Ireland's oldest recruitment web site. You can search for jobs by keyword or look at the various databases which cover for example agencies, companies, engineering, accounting, and graduates. You can browse by

**search jobs**

**Search for the perfe**
Let our extensive job
based on criteria you

**job agent**

**Let our agent do the**
Let our sophisticated
email when your perf

**career zone**

**Get expert advice**
Learn the tips, trick a
resume to sure-fire w

category, search by keyword and list by company. You can submit a résumé to either its IT or non-IT CV databases. They also have an IT worldwide section for employers/job seekers looking outside of Ireland. The site includes signposts to recruiters' jobs sites and profiles of recruitment agencies, a market report on current issues in recruitment, plus advice on CVs, interviews etc.

*Job Online (France)*
http://www.cegos.fr
This is the smart-looking French site of the Confédération Générale du Patronat Français, founded in 1926, to promote management and training in France. CEGOS has 750 associates and 500 consultants.

*Job Ware (Germany)*
http://www.jobware.de
This is a professional-looking online service designed for candidates seeking a job and companies seeking staff. The site is mainly in German of course, but international applicants can submit their details on its English-language international page.

*Jobs CZ (Czech Republic)*
http://www.jobs.cz
The site is all in Czech with no English translation facility.

*Jobs Vacatures op het Internet (Netherlands)*
http://www.jobs.nl
If you are looking for job opportunities in the Netherlands this is a good site to visit, but it is in Dutch only. The site contains a useful collection of local employment links.

*Le Monde (France)*
http://www.lemonde.fr
This is the online version of the French national daily newspaper, for which an English version is available. Look for job vacancies under 'L'espace emplois'.

*Lux (Luxembourg)*
http://www.luxweb.lu
This is an internet portal to Luxembourg. Follow the link to Jobs. The text is in French.

*Planet Recruit*
http://www.planetrecruit.com/channel/int/
This is one of the largest international and UK recruitment sites with over 80,000 jobs in over 80 countries – if you're looking for engineering jobs in England, IT in Ireland or sales in Sweden, PlanetRecruit.com should be able to find you the job you want.

*SmartJobb (Scandinavia)*
http://www.smartjobb.nu/

# Country information......................................................

This is a professional-looking resource for job-hunters wanting employment in Scandinavia. Get those Swedish and Norwegian dictionaries out, because there is no English on this site.

*Social Security System in Germany*
http://www.social-security.de
This one provides an excellent overview of the social security system in Germany that could be useful to expats living there.

*StepStone*
http://www.stepstone.co.uk
Fig. 37. StepStone has established itself as one of Europe's top online job sites.
This site – 'Europe's career portal' – includes vacancies across Europe and includes tips and articles, useful advice for applying to posts in some European countries including advice on international CVs and a job agent to search for jobs.

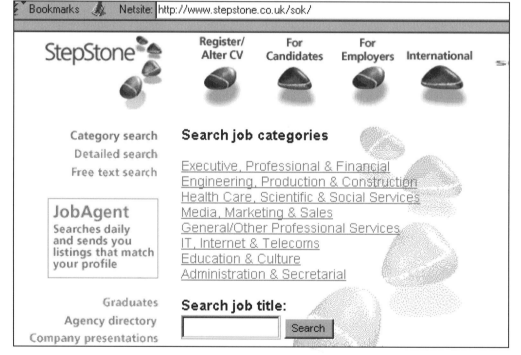

*Swiss Web Jobs*
http://www.swisswebjobs.ch
This is naturally a web site for jobs in Switzerland. It provides detailed links to employers, recruitment organisations, and offers various listings. The site is partly in German, and partly in French, but you will need to speak German to make full use of the service.

*Taps*
http://www.taps.com
TAPS is a Europe-wide recruitment agency, centred in Dublin, specialising in business, internet opportunities and graduates.

*The Job*
http://www.thejob.com
Thousands of jobs from across Europe are listed in this site. So whether you're experienced, or a graduate searching for your first placement, you should be able to find what you're looking for.

*UK Employment Service*
http://www.dfee.gov.uk/emp/
This is an official UK government site which includes information about European vacancies.

*Vacature Overzicht (Netherlands)*
http://www.iway.nl/intervac/
This site offers a comprehensive overview of jobs offered in Holland, updated every week. You will need your Dutch dictionary.

*Working in the EU*
http://www.cec.org.uk/pubs/facts/fact9701/working.htm
A useful information site about working in the European Union member states.

## Far East

*Access Asia*
http://www.accessasia.com
This site includes the Orient Business Express directory, which contains a million companies listed (this is a priced service but you can test-drive it). The site currently covers Hong Kong, Indonesia, Korea, Malaysia, the Philippines, Singapore, Taiwan, Thailand, China and India. There is also a set of web links.

Fig. 38. Asiadragons has evolved into a substantial regional jobs and search portal for 20 Asian countries including Australia and New Zealand. It is widely visited by travellers, businesses and students.

*Asiadragons Careers*
http://jobs.asiadragons.com/
This is a useful source of regular updates on Asian job and career opportunities. There are thousands of jobs from China and Hong Kong to Taiwan, Japan, Singapore and Malaysia.

*Asia Employment*
http://www.asia-employment.com
Check out this site for job search, employment and career opportunities for senior executives in Hong Kong, Singapore, China, Thailand, Indonesia, Japan, Korea and the Philippines.

*Asia Jobs*
http://www.asia-jobs.com
Here you can search for jobs in Asia, post résumés for recruiters to view, get salary information, and explore jobs news and trends.

Fig. 39. Asia Jobs.

*Asiaxpat*
http://www.asiaxpat.com
Operates expat sites covering a number of Asian cities. Check out your intended Asian destination.

*Career China*
http://www.dragonsurf.com/careerwise/
Visit this web site to explore some unusual career opportunities in China, Hong Kong, Taiwan, US and beyond.

*Career Mosaic Japan*
http://www.careermosaic.or.jp
This is a service from Career Mosaic, dedicated to services for Japan. It is in Japanese, so you will need to configure your web browser to view

Japanese characters. When reviewed, there was no facility to read the site in English.

*Contact Singapore*
http://www.contactsingapore.org.sg/
This is a useful site to visit if you want to work, live and study in Singapore.

*Daily Job (Hong Kong/China)*
http://www.dailyjob.com/
The site gets straight to the point, with listings in Hong Kong and China, updated daily. You can view 'today's vacancies' (about 30 when we reviewed the site) or look through the rather ambitious number of categories of jobs. However, you will be lucky to find a result to match the detailed search the site makes you perform. Job details are brief.

*ELT News (Japan)*
http://www.eltnews.com
This is an online newssheet for English language teaching in Japan. It contains current vacancies.

*Expat Expert*
http://www.expatexpert.com
This site is maintained by Robin Pascoe, a Canadian author, publisher, journalist, public speaker and international consultant on issues relating to the overseas living experience, especially in the Far East.

*Executive Asia*
http://www.executiveasia.com
Executive Asia is a head hunter and executive search firm specializing in IT and internet jobs throughout Hong Kong, Singapore, China and the Asia Pacific region.

*Expat Singapore*
http://www.expatsingapore.com
This is a huge city site for people living or moving to Singapore. It provides information arranged A to Z.

*Gemini Personnel (Hong Kong)*
http://www.gemini.com.hk
The Gemini Group was formed in Hong Kong in 1983. It says it is Hong Kong's leading recruitment company with hundreds of current vacancies, many of them with Hong Kong's multinationals. It handles all levels of placements in Hong Kong, Malaysia, Australia and London. The site includes company profile, salary surveys, an employment guide, an executive division, job search, candidate information, and a newsletter. It has separate divisions for information technology, banking and finance, engineering and construction, legal and professional, merchandising and general management. Overseas candidates are asked to read its online advice for non-Hong Kong job seekers.

*Guangzhou (China)*
http://www.nformd.com
Created by an expatriate spouse living in Guangzhou, the site offers lots of information for China hands.

*Hong Kong Jobs*
http://www.hkjobs.com
This site is dedicated to providing recruitment information in Hong Kong. With access to the largest online database for job openings in the territory, Hong Kong Jobs is capturing an increasingly larger share of the growing web audience.

*InterCareerNet (Japan)*
http://www.intercareer.com/japan/
InterCareer Net Japan provides employment information for job seekers who are fluent in English and Japanese. Candidates should either have, or plan to receive, a bachelor's or equivalent degree from an overseas university, or have experience working abroad. ICN-J is a service of International Career Information Inc, an international arm of Recruit Corporation in Tokyo. Site features include net job search, profile updating, careers fairs, links, candidates forum and membership information.

*Japan Career Agent*
http://japan.career-agent.net/
From here you can obtain a free daily email notification of jobs in Japan.

*Japan in Your Palm*
http://www.japaninyourpalm.com
Practical advice, in English, for expatriates planning to live and work in Japan.

*Japanese Jobs*
http://www.japanesejobs.com
This is a bilingual Japanese employment resource.

*Japanese Professional Job Site*
http://www.jpjs.co.uk
This is a résumé bank of Japanese bilingual professionals. You can register your résumé online free of charge. They will publish your details to the global business community, but your contact information remains confidential. JPJS will provide your contact information only to those companies registered with it. The service, which includes some recruiters and company site links, has been developed by the London-based Japanese MBA Club.

*JobAsia*
http://www.jobasia.com
In JobAsia you have access to three job search engines plus a search wizard to jobs in Hong Kong and other international cities. Jobs are classified into 36 job areas and more than 80 industries. You can save your

résumé in JobAsia and instantly submit your application online. Check out the company search, bulletin board, education centre, industry profiles and books.

*Job China*
http://jobchina.net/
With links to current job vacancies, and to Chinese recruitment organisations, this is a useful resource. You will find opportunities in Beijing, Xi'an, Guangzhou, Shenzhen and other major centres of enterprise.

*Jobs in Japan*
http://www.jobsinjapan.com
This is a new online guide to finding work and getting settled in.

*Living in Indonesia*
http://www.expat.or.id
If you are being assigned to Indonesia, or are presently living there, this site is well worth checking out. It includes general information about Indonesia, its economy, culture, people and daily practicalities, plus useful information and humorous stories about local expat life.

*Naukri (India)*
http://www.naukri.com
This is a really comprehensive resource for job seekers and employers in India. It includes more than 5,000 job leads less than 30 days old, links to placement agencies, major employers in India, and to more Indian career resources. There is also lots of careers advice. The site is updated twice a week. Based in Delhi, Naukri currently gets around 700,000 hits a month, making it the most popular Indian careers site by far. You can view the visitor statistics for yourself.

*Recruit Net*
http://www.recruit.net
This service focuses on IT jobs in Singapore, Hong Kong and Japan.

*Taiwan: Business Express*
http://business.com.tw
Here you can access a classified directory giving contact details, product area, and information such as capital for Taiwanese businesses.

*Teach in China*
http://teach-in-China.com
This is a bulletin board for posting openings for ESL/EFL teachers. There is a database of schools.

*Thailand Industrial Directory*
http://www.sino.net/thai/commerce/thaiprod.html
This site lists about 2,500 contacts, listed by sector by Trade Online Ltd. It gives basic contact details and some links to home pages.

*Welcome India*
http://www.welcomeindia.com/jobs/
This site offers extensive information and links on working in the US, Canada, Australia and New Zealand, as well as in the UK. You can also click onto seasonal and temporary work, careers information and contract work.

*Work In Japan*
http://www.workinjapan.com
Check out this site for jobs and careers in technology-related positions in Japan.

## The Middle East

*Arab Information Management Services*
http://www.aims-kw.com
AIMS was established in 1980 by two Kuwaiti businessmen. Today it is a leading Kuwaiti company in the information systems field with an annual turnover of US $15m.

*Arabian Careers*
http://www.arabiancareers.com
The company specialises in the recruitment of health care professionals for hospitals in Saudi Arabia.

*Bayt*
http://www.bayt.com
Bayt provides services to job seekers and employers throughout the Middle East. The site offers free CV posting, career advice, a CV builder, and a community forum covering regional lifestyles, workstyles, news and education.

Fig. 40. Career Mideast covers employment possibilities in the whole region from Bahrain to Yemen.

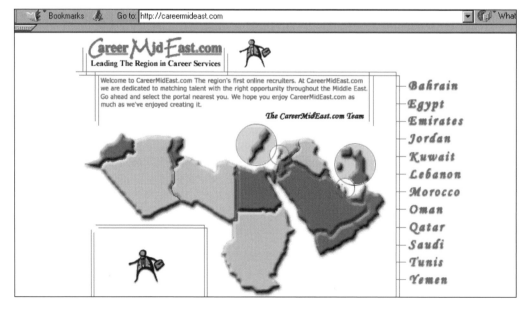

*Career MidEast*
http://careermideast.com
The site provides regional recruitment services for both employers and job seekers.

*Committee for Middle East Trade*
http://www.comet.org.uk
One of COMET's main objectives is to make British firms aware of the opportunities for doing business in Middle East markets. Its staff has extensive experience of the area and can advise on trading conditions in individual markets, provide sources of information about economic and development trends in the Middle East, and general aspects of trade policy.

*Kompass (United Arab Emirates)*
http://www.kompass-uae.com
This site offers a useful business database for the UAE.

*Saudijobs*
http://www.saudijobs.com
This is a placement consultant web site based in Saudi Arabia. Its contains available job listings.

*UAE Employment Pages*
http://www.uae-pages.com
The site includes a database of vacancies in the United Arab Emirates.

## North America

*ActiJob (Canada)*
http://www.actijob.com
From the home page of this site you can access hundreds of job opportunities in English or French. There are links to the job-chat centre and further employment and recruitment sites.

*American Chamber of Commerce*
http://www.amcham.org.uk
AMCHAM was established in 1916 and for more than 80 years has helped its members to competitively build their international businesses. It is a non-profit organisation and reinvests its cash in programmes for its members.

*American Jobs*
http://www.americanjobs.com
The site offers a free searchable database of hi-tech computer and engineering jobs with Fortune 500 companies and leading corporations. It was launched in 1994 and apparently logs up a staggering 2 million hits each month. Its online employer profiles enable you to conduct research on several hundred employers currently posting jobs on the site. This extensive background information will help you to determine which companies are right for you. You can add your résumé to its off-line

**-A-**

* **AAA Ohio**
* **AT&T Wireless**
* **Abacus Staffing**
* **Adea Group**
* **Adecco**
* **Advanced Altern**
* **Advanced Const**
* **Advanced Mortg**
* **Advanced Syste**
* **Advanced Techr**
* **Aetea**
* **Advanced Hardv**
* **AlaWeb Internet**
* **Allard Programr**
* **Allenetics Exect**

database where they say your privacy is assured. The site says it will never submit your résumé to any company or individual without your permission.

### American Recruitment
http://www.americanrecruitment.com
This is a contact point for sales, marketing and retail jobs, mainly in California.

### America's Employers
http://www.americasemployers.com
Developed by the Career Relocation Corporation of America, the site is based on the outplacement and job-finding assistance programs it has provided to many Fortune 500 companies for over fifteen years. Whether you are unemployed, considering a career move, or just keeping your options open, you can use its resources to organise, expand and refine your own job search. It includes a company database, job search, a résumé bank, entrepreneurial options, career chat, relocation resources such as salary and mortgage calculators, and other job-hunting advice and information.

### America's Job Bank
http://www.ajb.dni.us
The AJB network is a national clearing-house for the public employment service. Around 5,000 new jobs are received from the different States each day. Additionally, thousands of employers enter their jobs directly into the system in real time. On average, more than 3,000 new jobs are received each day directly from employers. You can search the national jobs file or any of the state job banks, but you need to register in order to submit a résumé to AJB and save your own custom searches.

### Art Job
http://www.webart.com/artjob
Established for nineteen years, this is an American newsletter issued online every two weeks, containing job listings in the arts fields. They include academic, agencies, artistic performance, conferences, international, internships, presenting and producing organisations, publications, and special features of interest. Sample listings are available, as well as subscription information.

### AWE Recruitment
http://www.awe-recruitment.freeserve.co.uk/
This company provides European staff for US children's summer camps. AWE stands for American Work Experience.

### Bank Jobs (USA)
http://www.bankjobs.com/
This is a massive specialist American site for banking jobs. When we reviewed it we found it had 10,696 banking-related jobs online, plus many ancillary services, and numerous banking links.

Fig. 41. Best Jobs in the USA today is a substantial careers employment portal.

*Best Jobs in the USA Today*

http://www.bestjobsusa.com

The site describes itself as a premier employment magazine. It offers a career guide with job opportunities, career fairs and advice, résumé posting, workplace information, and company profiles. You can do a keyword search to locate thousands of positions by city, skills, position, selecting from many industries such IT, engineering, finance, business, health care and others. You can also follow a vast number of A-Z links to other employment-related sites, research a US city, access unemployment rates and cost-of-living information, population, major employers, and get a briefing on each city's economic status. Each company profiles itself, and you can access current job listings direct.

*Britain in the USA*

http://www.britain-info.org

This site includes some useful fact sheets about employment and UK immigration. The information has been put together by the British Embassy.

*Canada Employment Weekly*

http://www.mediacorp2.com

*Canada Employment Weekly* is Canada's largest career newspaper. This online edition brings you some of the 500 vacancies available each week, well organised into various categories. The site also features a career directory where you can match your qualifications with 900 Canadian employers, plus 'Who's Hiring' which ranks 4,000 of Canada's top employers in 23 occupations. This valuable site is a project of Toronto-based Mediacorp Canada Inc.

*Canada Industry Online: Strategis*
http://strategis.ic.gc.ca
This is a good site maintained by Industry Canada, a government agency. It includes monthly economic indicators, provincial overviews (business activity and prospects), statistical industry overviews, detailed information on key industry sectors, and a section on advanced technologies. It also has a directory of thousands of Canadian companies including contact details, employee numbers, product type and good list of company directory links (particularly Canadian, but also some others).

Fig. 42. Canada Jobs has vacancies for everyone from agriculture workers to X-ray technicians, and for those looking for either high-tech or non-computer jobs. It links to JobBus, another big Canadian jobs web site.

*Canada Jobs*
http://www.canadajobs.com
This is a useful collection of links to job databases, government job banks, newsgroups, employment agencies and companies that have Canadian job listings on their homepages.

*Canadian Job Catalogue*
http://www.kenevacorp.mb.ca
Canadian Job Catalogue offers literally thousands of links to job sites, information and résumé banks with Canadian content. These sites are sorted into categories for easy reference. For example, there are over 65 major Canadian job and résumé banks containing thousands of postings, plus over 400 smaller one containing thousands more. There are more than 1,100 Canadian occupation or industry specific sites giving free access to thousands of Canadian job postings under more than 90 separate categories, plus many regional sub-categories. The Catalogue also has Canadian job listings not on the net: local telephone hot lines and speciality associations with job openings. You can also find some 140 sites offering help and information on Canadian interview techniques, top employers/expanding companies, résumé creation and emailing, career planning, career training, employment law, employment news,

helpful resources, and labour market information. If you feel Canada calling, this site is a must.

*Career Bridge (Canada)*
http://www.careerbridge.com
Career Bridge has offices in Ottawa and Toronto. Its Career Centre is the place to begin if you are looking for employment opportunities. Before accessing the full site, you prepare and post your résumé to the internet, using the résumé entry wizard. You can then browse a database of jobs posted by employers, apply online and communicate with potential employers through your personal message centre, all for free. You can edit your résumé at any time. There are even occasional career opportunities with Career Bridge itself. The site contains profiles of about 70 leading organisations posting vacancies on the site, including such well-known names as Andersen Consulting, the Bank of Nova Scotia, and the Royal College of Physicians & Surgeons of Canada.

*Career Builder (USA)*
http://www.careerbuilder.com
The USA Career Builder network brings together several leading career sites on one site for a targeted search. For job hunters there are free job notifications, a personal search agent to deliver jobs to you, hot companies, news about Microsoft and CACI, companies on Career Builder, an A-Z list of every company posting jobs to Career Builder, relocation resources, a salary calculator, apartment search, metro guides and more. For employers there is stuff on the benefits of online recruiting, targeting the perfect hire, posting jobs to USA Today, Medical Economics, Developer.com and more than a dozen other career sites. The company has offices in major cities across the USA.

*Career City (USA)*
http://www.careercity.com
This is an impressive and in depth American careers site. You can search jobs in all professions, refine your search, find out about regional job fairs, prepare and post résumés, and check out employers programs. In the computer/hi-tech careers centre there are job listings, links to 3,000+ hi-tech firms, salary surveys, resources and hi-tech agencies. A section on companies and industries gives information on 27,000 US employers, 7,000 employment services, 1,000 temp firms, with links to 1,000s of resources for hi-tech careers, government careers, health care careers and education careers.

*Career Connections (USA)*
http://www.career.com/
This in-depth US employment site has home page links to job seekers, employers, hot jobs, what's new, and more. You can create, save and update your résumé. Other resources include personal career assessment, where an in-depth appraisal will provide you with a mirror of your vocational strengths. You can also download and try its all-new edition of 'Wanted Jobs', a free job-finding tool you can use to search up to 32

job sites including this one. The site also offers 'power tools for relocation' comprising a salary calculator, moving calculator, relocation planning, an auto/home insurance wizard and mortgage qualifier program. The salary calculator, for example, tells you how much you would need to make in your new city to keep your current lifestyle.

*Career Internetworking (Canada)*
http://www.careerkey.com/
Career Internetworking is a Canadian online career networking resource, based in Ontario, for professionally and technically qualified applicants. Its free services include resources, strategies, tips, profiles and an open communication forum. You can browse job opportunities in Canadian manufacturing and distribution industries and meet leading companies through its 'jobs and profiles' section. Web pages, complete web sites or links to existing home pages give you company news, policies, commitments, future plans, products and services, upcoming events, plus jobs. The employers post vacancies for a 30-day period. There are sections on what's new, latest jobs, new career search, hot jobs, search by location, position, category, key contacts and online career assistance, job search tips and articles. There are some very friendly applicant-oriented FAQs on the site.

*Career Magazine (USA)*
http://www.careermag.com
*Career Magazine* is a comprehensive and attractively presented resource, designed for job seekers. It downloads and indexes job postings from the major internet newsgroups every day. Postings are searchable by location, job title and/or skills required. It also runs a résumé bank, which gives recruiters a tool to locate résumés of suitable candidates. Candidates can enter résumé information into this bank using an online form. For candidates, there are employer profiles, offering detailed information on employers around the world. There are products and services to help you manage your career, articles and news to help you plan and execute your networked career search, plus the career forum – a moderated discussion area.

*Career Mart (USA)*
http://www.careermart.com/
This is another all purpose USA jobs site. Like many others it offers online job search, company profiles, email service, job advertising and résumé posting. The job search page took a while to load but it offered the ability to search by job categories, states, regions and international (which included the UK). The A to Z list of companies also took a long while to load, because it contained a massive number of company links in a single page, but once loaded it was easy to navigate and use.

*Career Path (USA)*
http://www.careerpath.com
Career Path was co-founded in October 1995 by six major American newspapers, *The Boston Globe, Chicago Tribune, Los Angeles Times, The*

*New York Times, San Jose Mercury-News* and *The Washington Post*. On this site you can search the job ads of all these newspapers, search job postings gathered from leading employers' web sites, post a confidential résumé, gather information on featured employers, check out upcoming job fairs, and explore career spotlights. Career Path claims to offer job seekers the greatest number of the most current jobs available – some 263,000 when we reviewed the site. No listing remains on its database for more than two weeks, so the vacancies really are current.

*Career Paths Online (Canada)*
http://careerpathsonline.com
This is the internet version of *Career Paths Newspaper*, an official Canadian career planning guide for designed to help students and young people formulate their career and education plans.

*Career Spot (USA)*
http://www.careerspot.com
This is a gateway to over 8,000 jobs in south Florida. The site is a service of *The Sun-Sentinel* newspaper, and the site can take you to lots of associated classified advertising, such as for cars and apartments, should you be contemplating a move to the Sunshine State.

*Career Web (USA)*
http://www.cweb.com
This is a mainly American database containing over 20,000 job openings from more than 300 companies. The home page leads you more or less straight into search mode – for jobs, or for employers. The results did not appear to be in any particular order, but they were numbered for ease of reference. You can also research employers and get lots of job searching advice. This site's listings cover engineering, information systems, telecommunications, marketing, accounting, healthcare, and many more categories. Companies helpfully listed in bold type have profile pages with corporate, product and employee benefits information for you to review. You can also put your résumé in their database and refer it to employers. Its job match service will notify you by email about job opportunities that match the type of job and location you're looking for. Other site features also include a career inventory section, career doctor, and bookstore (which takes the form of another searchable database).

*Careers Boston (USA)*
http://www.careers.boston.com
Careers Boston contains New England's largest database of jobs, with more than 15,000 employment opportunities weekly. Online listings are added daily. *Boston Sunday Globe* listings are updated every Monday.

*Companies Online*
http://www.companiesonline.com
Here you will find a Dun and Bradstreet/Lycos directory of US companies – search by state, city, industry, company name. The site also

offers links to company web sites.

*Contract Employment Weekly*
http://www.ceweekly.com
Established in the USA in 1969, *Contract Employment Weekly* has been
an electronic magazine since 1994. It contains lots of highly paid technical, IT and engineering contract assignments available from 500
agencies in its online database. Between 3,000 and 4,000 listings are
updated every 30 minutes. About a quarter of these are viewable by
non-subscribers. A contract worker is typically a highly qualified, highly
paid individual who works for a contract service firm on temporary job
assignment for that firm's client company. The average length of the
assignment is six to nine months.

*E Jobs (USA/Canada)*
http://www.ejobs.org
This is a handy source of information on environmental jobs and careers,
developed by an American environmental analyst. It includes careers
such as environmental engineers, nature and wetlands scientists, GIS,
technicians, chemists, geologists, geotechnical experts, policy and law,
wildlife conservation, land use planning, and education.

*E-CV (US)*
http://www.e-cv.com
With links to its international sites, this US–based company offers to
send your résumé and cover letter directly to thousands of qualified
hiring professionals via electronic networking. Their database consists
of over 10,000 hiring companies and professionals.

Fig. 43. The impressive
US-based Headhunter
web site also includes an
International Gateway
area.

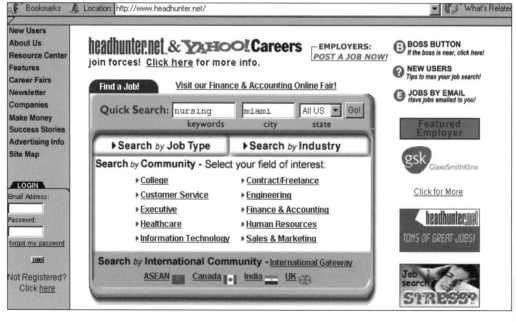

*Elstead Maps (USA)*
http://www.elstead.co.uk/usawrk.htm
USA Working Abroad Guides are offered through this home page.

*Head Hunter (USA)*
http://www.headhunter.net
The statistics on this site seem pretty staggering – over 250,000 job listings online, over 64,000 jobs updated this week, 70,000 résumés online, and 60,000 different users per day. The database is said to be constantly cleaned: jobs are never over 45 days old, and résumés are never over 90 days old. It offers free basic posting, with a third of jobs posted by companies, and two thirds by recruiters. Given the sheer volume of notified vacancies, the site is well worth a visit.

*HiTech Career Center (Canada)*
http://www.hitechcareer.com
This is an informative careers resource for IT jobs in Canada, produced by Kaplan Career Services which says it is the largest provider of career forums and services in North America. The site contains details of careers fairs in Toronto, Ottawa, Calgary, Montreal, and Vancouver.

*Job Bank (USA)*
http://www.jobbankusa.com
This is a well-known award-winning American site, with a comprehensive directory of internet employment resources. These include a powerful job meta-search page by which you can access the internet's

Fig. 44. Located in Florida, Job Bank USA has grown into one of the internet's largest and best-known online recruiting sites, having provided services to over 5 million job seekers and hiring managers since 1995.

largest employment databases. Job hunters can search jobs, submit/edit résumés, use job scout (an email agent), check out hot-list firms and employment newsgroups, find out about career fairs, and use assessment and relocation tools. With its international search services, you can quickly find people, businesses, and other information all over the world, including the UK and Europe. Employers are invited to become members and gain access to its résumé database.

### Job Connection (USA)
http://www.jobconnection.com
This USA service comprises around 200 recruiting firms who operate on a national, regional, state, and local basis.

### Job Lynx (USA)
http://joblynx.com
Job Lynx says it can place your details before more than 12,000 professional recruiters who are actively searching for thousands of job candidates. Confidentiality is guaranteed, as only headhunters have access to your résumé. The database is set up so that only registered headhunters with an assigned password can access it. Resumer posters are charged fees, depending on membership option and period of posting.

### JobSat (Canada)
http://www.jobsat.com
This is a free service for job seekers looking for employment in Canada and select US locations. You can do résumé posting or use the job search section of over 8,500 job listings. The résumé posting section is a free web based posting service available to all users. The Job Search section is available to registered users only. You will need to register for best access. JobSat offers recruiters the Lite Viewer, a management tool to expedite the matching of job seekers with suitable employers. It screens out applicants based on criteria input by the user, who does not have to waste valuable time skimming through thousands of résumés/job postings. It also allows for access to Jobsat's database.

### Job Search California (USA)
http://www.jsearch.com
This site maintains databases of 40,000 companies, over 100,000 current news stories, more than 2,000 résumé summaries and 5,000 active job postings throughout southern California. It includes some rather crude self-evaluation tests for candidates. We completed one as a test (21 questions) and were told we had skills in mentoring, synthesizing diverting, negotiating, coordinating, instructing, innovating, supervising, analysing, compiling, persuading, computing, speaking, copying, signalling, comparing, serving, taking, instructions, and helping. Well, its what we always thought!

### Job Source Network (USA)
http://www.jobsourcenetwork.com
This is another impressive and in-depth USA site with links to thousands

of job sites world wide. You can do a job search, select job categories, countries of the world, and your favourite search engines, using handy drop down lists. Another main feature of the site is the huge number of job listings in major US newspapers, which you can trawl through by name in a long drop-down menu. The site is a project of Benjamin Scott Publishing, Washington DC.

*Job Trak (USA)*
http://www.jobtrak.com
Based in Los Angeles, this is another US-based employment site, intended primarily for college students and alumni. With over 35,000 visitors per day and 3,000 new job openings daily, it is one of the larger employment sites on the internet. Over the past ten years it has formed partnerships with some 800 college career centres. It offers a worthwhile source of information and links to graduate employers in the States. You will find a job search manual, and vacancies for part-time jobs, temp jobs and internships. Job Trak says that, since 1987, over 300,000 employers have used its services to target students and alumni from their choice of campuses. The fee to advertisers ranges from $18 per campus up to $395 for all 800 schools.

- ▶ Find a Job
- ▶ Register & Post
- ▶ JobTalk Message
- ▶ Career Contact &
- ▶ Online Career Fai
- ▶ Employer Showca
- ▶ Jobtrak Academy
- ▶ Jobs @ Jobtrak
- ▶ Job Search Tips

*Job Web (USA)*
http://www.jobweb.com
Job Web is a project of the National Association of Colleges and Employers. It has 1,700 member universities and colleges drawn from across the United States (and their career services professionals), and 1,600 employer organisations in the private sector. Also represented are numerous federal, state, and local governmental agencies and their HR/employment professionals. Job Web says it serves over a million college students and alumni who use its publications and services every year.

*National Business Employment Weekly*
http://careers.wsj.com
This is a US-based career guidance and job search publication. Subscribers are promised the latest on business and franchising opportunities. The site includes an index for job hunters outside the US as well as feature articles, archive and special discount information.

*Net Jobs (Canada)*
http://www.netjobs.com
Net Jobs is a Canadian employment site. The jobs are listed under such categories as computer programming, engineering and technical, graphic design and arts, information systems, programmers and analysts, management information systems, networking and network design, sales and marketing, technical sales, and the transportation industry.

*Occupational Outlook Handbook (USA)*
http://stats.bls.gov/ocohome.htm
The *Occupational Outlook Handbook* is a basic reference source for careers and employment in the USA. You can use this web site to find

# Country information .................................................................

information about specific occupations, perform a keyword search on the handbook, use the index to the handbook, and select from an occupational cluster. The handbook is published by the US Bureau of Labor Statistics.

Fig. 45. Seasonal Employment is a small but focused online service which offers short-term job possibilities for both the USA and Canada.

*Seasonal Employment*
http://www.seasonalemployment.com
This is an ever-growing database of seasonal employers in the USA and Canada.

| | ress | 🖉 | http://www.SeasonalEmployment.com/state.html | | | ▾ | ⌀ Go | Link |

| Company Name, Website &/or Email | Address | Phones | FAXes | Hires People per Season, Duration, etc. | Elevation &/or Climate |
|---|---|---|---|---|---|
| **Grand Canyon National Park Lodges** the Grand Canyon is one of the 'Seven Wonders of the World' | PO Box 699, Grand Canyon, AZ 86023-9989 | (520) 638-2343 | ~~~ | ALOT: for a season, a year or a career. Apr - Oct RV sites available | 7,000' to 9,000' |
| **Lake Powell Resorts & Marinas** Glen Canyon Nat'l Rec Area bingham-inta@aramark.com | PO Box 1597, Page, AZ 86040 {AZ & UT} | (520) 645-1081 | (520) 645-1016 | 1,200 Apr thru Nov RV sites available | 3,700' 100+ degrees HOT & DRY |
| **DNPS - Sequoia** seqpark@inreach.com | PO Box 89, 64740 Wuksachi Way, Sequoia NP, CA 93262 | (559) 565-0340 | (559) 565-0334 | 100 - 250 mid Apr - Oct RV sites are limited | 7,000' to 9,000' |
| **Paramount's Great America** Theme Park | Attn: Empl. Dept., 2401 Agnew Rd., Santa Clara, CA 95054 | ~~~ | (408) 986-5950 | 2,900 See **Multi States** below also! ALL Year | ~~~ |
| **Sequoia-Kings Canyon Park Services Co** jmorris@sequoia-kingscanyon.com | 5755 E Kings Canyon Rd, Suite 101, Fresno, | (559) 452-1000 | (559) 452-1353 | 150 May - Oct RV sites are limited | 4,000' to 7,000' |

*Top Jobs USA*
http://www.topjobsusa.com
This is a very extensive database of job listings concentrated on the western United States, such as Arizona, California, Colorado, Idaho, Nevada, New Mexico, Oregon, Texas, and Utah. It claims to contain over 50,000 job listings. You can submit your résumé. There is also quite a detailed links section, leading you to such further resources as US academic institutions, chambers of commerce, government sources, recruiting agencies, careers advice pages, other internet job lists, résumé banks, search engines and numerous other categories.

## South America and the Caribbean

*Caribbean Job Fair*
http://www.caribbeanjobfair.com/
This is believed to be the first and only web site that focuses solely on matching supply and demand in the Caribbean labour market, spanning the islands and countries within the region. Updated on a daily basis, the site offers vacancies, résumés and labour market related news and updates which relate to the Caribbean.

*Expat Village (Argentina)*
http://www.expatvillage.com
This is a site for expatriates in Buenos Aires, Argentina

*LatPro*
http://www.LatPro.com
This is the web site of the Latin American Professional's Network. It announces employment opportunities and information for bilingual and bicultural professionals from the Americas. LatPro is not itself an executive recruiter, but a 13,000-strong membership organisation linking its members and corporate and executive recruiters searching for bilingual (Spanish or Portuguese and English) professionals. It contains job announcements for people with Spanish and Portuguese language skills, links to the Latin American countries, and other resources. You can pay a small membership fee to receive email announcements.

# 9 Industry-specific job sites

**In this chapter we will explore:**

▶ *au pairs*
▶ *electronics and IT*
▶ *energy industries*
▶ *engineering and construction*
▶ *entertainment industry*
▶ *health care*
▶ *hospitality, travel and tourism*
▶ *languages*
▶ *management and professional*
▶ *maritime*
▶ *public services*
▶ *science*
▶ *teaching*

## Au pairs

*Au Pair Job Match*
http://www.aupairs.co.uk
This is an automated job matching service for au pairs and families. You can register free of charge and have your details forwarded to matching families or au pairs. There are advertised vacancies from agencies and employers, and a discussion forum. You can read the site in several different European languages.

*Childcare International*
http://www.childint.co.uk
This site offers a service to families looking for an au pair or nanny and for potential au pairs or nannies looking for a placement. They have links in UK, Europe, Canada and US.

## Electronics and IT

*AEA Japan*
http://www.aea.or.jp
The American Electronics Association represents the electronics, software and IT industries in Japan. Its web site offers access to US-Japan trade agreements, a list of member companies and links to high-tech job sources for Japan. Your browser needs to be able to handle Japanese characters for some of this site.

*Elan*
http://www.elan.co.uk
Elan is a specialist IT and communications recruitment consultancy with a network of offices spanning the UK, Europe, Asia and the USA.

*Eclectic International*
http://www.peoplesoft-recruitment.com
Kestrel Consulting is a global recruitment firm specialising in the recruitment and placement of SAP, Peoplesoft, JD Edwards and client server experienced professionals throughout the world.

*Jobs in Telecoms*
http://www.jobsintelecoms.com
Jobs in Telecoms is a specialist recruitment web site for the international telecoms industry. You can find information on permanent, contract and temporary telecoms vacancies in the UK and Europe.

*IntaPeople*
http://www.intapeople.co.uk
The site offers contract and permanent IT jobs. Most are in the UK, but there are a few to be found on mainland Europe as well.

*Jobs Worldwide*
http://www.jobsworldwide.co.uk
You can search for IT jobs worldwide with this UK 'search and selection' agency. It's early days yet, but its database of vacancies should eventually have jobs in Australia, New Zealand, Canada, USA, Europe and the UK.

*Lateral Solutions*
http://www.lateral-solutions.com
Based in Bracknell, Berkshire, Lateral Solutions is part of the Hamilton Parker International group of companies, representing the whole range of recruitment solutions, from executive search to outsourcing. It provides permanent and contract recruitment to the IT, electronic engineering, mobile phone and telecommunications industries worldwide.

*Total Systems Resourcing*
http://www.tsr.co.uk
This IT recruitment agency has jobs for software engineers, analyst programmers, technical support engineers and project leaders – both in this country and abroad.

## Energy industries

*Alba International*
http://www.alba.net
Alba is a recruitment and contracting company to the major oil and gas companies throughout the world from its head office in the Isle of Man, with offices in Azerbaijan, Kuwait and Malaysia. You can visit these pages to explore opportunities in oil and gas recruitment worldwide. Alba has a computerised database of over 8,000 fully qualified and experienced oil and gas personnel to cover the requirements of the industry.

# Industry-specific job sites ..................................................

*Videotel Marine International*
http://www.videotel.co.uk
From the home page, you can link into video and computer training packages for the marine industry, offshore oil and gas-related sectors and safety packages for other selected industries.

## Engineering and construction

Fig. 46. Careers in Construction offers a variety of employment opportunities abroad for architects, consultants, contractors, surveyors and other qualified professionals.

*Careers in Construction*
http://www.careersinconstruction.com
From the home page of this site, you can access jobs (architecture, consultants, contractors, surveyors), CV service, offshore jobs, training and resources for freelancers. The site is run by the UK publishing group EMAP.

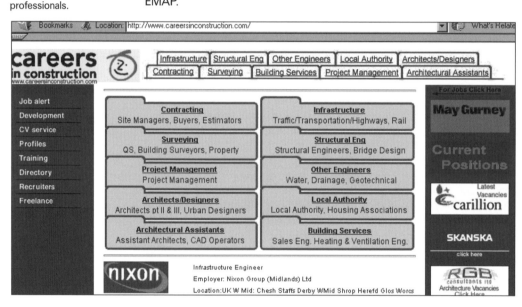

*Earthworks*
http://ourworld.compuserve.com/homepages/eworks/
You will find careers, jobs and training opportunities for all disciplines related to earth sciences including ecology, geocomputing, archaeology, oceanography, mining and astronomy plus more on this site.

## Entertainment industry

*Entertainment Employment Journal*
http://www.eej.com
Since 1992, the Entertainment Employment Journal has been serving the career needs of thousands of professional, creative, technical, production personnel and others interested in a career in the motion picture, broadcast or cable television business. Twice a month, subscribers are informed about full-time positions and internships. The site includes a US directory of entertainment employers. Companies are listed alphabetically and by location and are organised into more than 40 major categories.

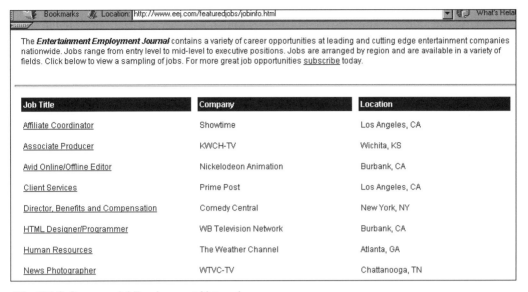

Fig. 47. The web site of the Entertainment Employment journal.

*Film, TV, & Commercial Employment Network*
http://www.employnow.com
This American network provides important information and resources for individuals interested in pursuing a career in the entertainment industry. It's for beginners as well as seasoned professionals. Information and resources are provided for many areas both behind and in front of the camera. If you're a producer or casting director, you can visit 'Actors Now' to view photos and résumés of talented performers. If you're wanting to break into the business, check out the employment guide or the production assistant's handbook. There are quite a few detailed job listings, stuff for actors, screen writers and comedians, plus industry links.

*Hollywood Creative Directory*
http://www.hcdonline.com
This organisation publishes industry guides relating to many areas of film and television, from agents and managers to producers and distributors and many more. Its materials may be purchased in printed form, or subscribed to online.

*Screen Actors Guild*
http://www.sag.com
This is the official web site of the Screen Actors Guild. It explains the qualifications you would need for joining this actors' union. While multi-million dollar movie deals make headlines for some stars, creating a false impression that all actors are highly paid, the reality is far less glamorous. According to the Guild's statistics, in 1996 more than 80 per cent of its 90,000 members earned less than $5,000. But if you feel you have what it takes to break into this competitive field, this is good place to start. To join, you must show proof of employment or prospective employment within two weeks or less by a Guild signatory company, and pay a joining fee of around $1,200.

# Industry-specific job sites ............................................

*Showbiz Jobs*
http://www.showbizjobs.com
Showbiz Jobs is a Hollywood-based membership organisation of recruitment managers from leading companies in the film, television, recording and attractions industries seeking candidates for a multitude of industry-related positions. This well organised site includes a Jobs Board where you can look at current career opportunities with the entertainment leaders for free. You can search by company name, job category, or geographic location for the latest job openings. There are plenty of vacancies. Responding is as easy as emailing your CV direct to the respective recruitment offices. There is a $35 fee to submit your résumé for a six-month period.

*Theatre Jobs*
http://theatrejobs.com
This is a well-organised online job search system serving the North American entertainment industry. The ads are free, but as a job seeker you will have to subscribe. When we reviewed the site we found 465 job listings online. You can learn more about theatre jobs including additional services, special subscription rates, explore links to interesting theatre sites, and join the theatre jobs mailing list to receive notices of hot jobs, and discount prices.

*TV Jobs*
http://www.tvjobs.com
TV Jobs provides North American employment information, résumés, jobs, professional development, station information and other resources for the professional broadcaster. It also includes a Worldwide Freelance Directory containing a searchable database of professional freelancers. TV Jobs has some 1,600 broadcasting stations organised into a fully searchable index. It looks to be a pretty comprehensive and interesting site with enormous amounts of information of value to anyone seeking to develop their career in this market.

## Health care

*Medical Ad Mart*
http://www.medical-admart.com
Medical Ad Mart's pages contain advertisements for positions, products and services for the medical professional. It has compiled and brought online the best selection of classified advertising pages drawn from leading USA medical journals, such as *American Family Physician, California Physician, Regional Anesthesia,* and *Veterinary Forum*.

*Medical Employment Services*
http://www.med-employ.com
Medical Employment Services is a USA service based on email, not web pages. Messages about new medical and nursing employment opportunities can be sent to appropriate potential candidates within a few hours of the time they are sent to the site.

*MediStaff*
http://www.medistaff.com
MediStaff are California-based specialists in the placement of physical therapists, PTAs, occupational therapists, registered nurses and speech language pathologists, into permanent and travelling positions across America. There are also some opportunities in the UK and in Saudi Arabia. The service is a division of World Wide Staffing Inc based in Vancouver, Canada.

*MedSearch*
http://www.medsearch.com
MedSearch is a career centre, bulletin board, newsgroup and employment site all rolled into one. With access to and data on employment opportunities, strategic partnerships, professional alliances, mergers, acquisitions, industry trends, and other issues shaping the future of health care, MedSearch provides a whole range of professional support, including a database of jobs in the medical and healthcare industries. You can also submit your résumé into their database via an online form, or send it to them by email. This very professional looking site offers a pretty comprehensive coverage of the US medical and health care fields. Its international jobs section contained more than 500 vacancies for Europe.

Fig. 48. Medsearch is now part of the Monster online jobs network, run by TMP Worldwide.

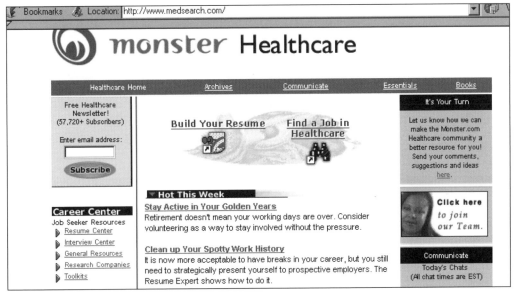

*World Healthcare Exchange*
http://www.whe.co.uk
WHE is geared towards healthcare professionals such as nurses, occupational therapists, physiotherapists and doctors who want to work abroad.

▶ See also – *Medicine & Health on the Internet* (Internet Handbooks).

## Hospitality, travel and tourism

*Aviation Employee Placement Service*
http://www.aeps.com
This specialist site says that it is used by more than 2,800 aviation companies worldwide. You are invited to enter your qualifications with a free ten-day trial. You can receive free email job alerts by entering your email address. For full facilities you must enrol as a member. The company is based in Fort Lauderdale, Florida.

*Fresh-Tracks*
http://www.fresh-tracks.co.uk/app/fresh/Forms/Freshframe.htm
This London-based ski recruitment agency offers on-line CV registration, advice on how to get a job and information about the European ski resorts.

*Grant International*
http://www.ttg.co.uk/grant/
Grant provides recruitment services to the international hotel and leisure industries. It employs various recruitment methods including executive search, database selection and direct advertising to ensure the right people from pastry chefs to directors. A handful of vacancies are detailed on the site, which is connected with *The Travellers' Guide*.

*Hospitality Jobs Online*
http://www.hjo.net
Hospitality Jobs Online is dedicated to select market segments of the travel and tourism industry. It provides internet recruiting services to hotels, food and beverage establishments, travel groups, casinos, and cruise lines. The site is presented in affiliation with the Los Angeles Hotel Human Resources Association.

*Hospitality Net*
http://www.hospitalitynet.org
This is another USA internet resource for the global hospitality industry – 'all of hospitality on the web'. You can click on a couple of dozen job categories to find a position that might suit your requirements. As a test we searched for jobs in Catering & Convention Management, and found 26 vacancies. Each had a hyperlink to detailed job descriptions and contact details for applicants. You can also check out their employer listings. Posting entries is free to employers who register not more than 10 entries per month. The site appears to be updated weekly.

*Hotel Jobs*
http://www.hoteljobs.com
They say: 'Find a greater job by searching the hoteljobs.com job openings database or specify the job you are seeking and have us email you when new job opportunities are posted.' The site includes a messageboard and email alert, and you can post your CV here.

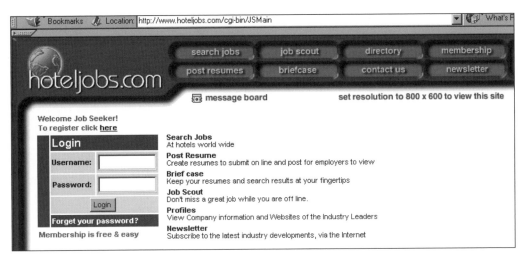

*Humana International Group*

http://www.humana-pm.com

Humana has been part of the world's largest executive search organisation, since early 1995. It provides a specialist service to the hotel, hospitality and leisure sectors throughout the world. It handles general management positions, department heads and above at hotel unit level, all positions at corporate level especially MD, FD, and operations directors. It covers all disciplines to include rooms, food and beverage, finance, IT, sales and marketing, property management, human resources and purchasing. It also handles senior consultancy within the hospitality sector. Its clients include the multinationals, medium and small organisations, independent hotels, and leading consultancies. You can submit your CV, and search its database using keywords, and selecting various international locations.

*Travel Training Company*

http://www.tttc.co.uk

The Travel Training Company is the principal provider of training and qualifications for anybody looking for a career in travel or already working within the travel industry.

*VIP Personnel*

http://www.vipstaff.com.au

VIP is an established (30 years) Australian hospitality recruitment specialist, listing jobs available in Australia and South East Asia. Based in Melbourne, it recruits casual and permanent placement of staff at all levels of the hospitality industry. It claims to have the largest database of hospitality professionals in the southern hemisphere. Some of the job listings seemed to be rather out of date.

▶ See also – *Travel & Holidays on the Internet* by Graham Jones (Internet Handbooks).

Fig. 49. Hotel Jobs. Its Job Scout service will track down vacancies for you even while you are offline.

# Industry-specific job sites ............................................

## Languages

*Gateway Greece*
http://www.gatewaygreece.com
This site offers advice on teaching in Greek schools. It explains the quali-fications needed, the going rate for the job and dealing with bureaucracy. It is run by Michael Reid, an English teacher from Britain, who has lived and worked there for six years.

*Institute of Linguistics*
http://www.iol.org.uk
You can link into vacancy listings and information on qualifications.

Fig. 50. Based in central London, Merrow has 35 years' experience in multilingual recruitment.

*Merrow*
http://www.merrow.co.uk
This consultancy specialises in the recruitment of multi-lingual staff.

## Management and professional

*Hamilton Recruitment*
http://www.hamilton-recruitment.com
These people recruit chartered accountants from the UK & North Amer-ica to work in the world's premier financial centres such as Bermuda, the Caribbean and the Channel Islands. Earn a tax-free salary and enjoy an outstanding quality of life in these exciting international locations.

*LPA Legal Recruitment*
http://www.the-lpa.co.uk
This is the web site of a London-based legal recruitment agency which places lawyers at firms throughout the UK and abroad. You can submit your CV online.

*O'Connell Associates*
http://www.oconnell.co.uk
This is a firm of recruitment consultants for the financial services sector. It has links with executive search firms worldwide and lists high-powered vacancies on various continents, along with profiles of individuals in the market for new jobs.

## Maritime

*Crewseekers International Yacht Crew and Sailing Services*
http://www.crewseekers.co.uk
This is one of the premier yacht crew introduction agencies in Europe.

Fig. 51. Crewseekers includes both amateur and professional crew of all ages and experience who share a keen interest in sailing. Beginners and experts alike are welcome to join.

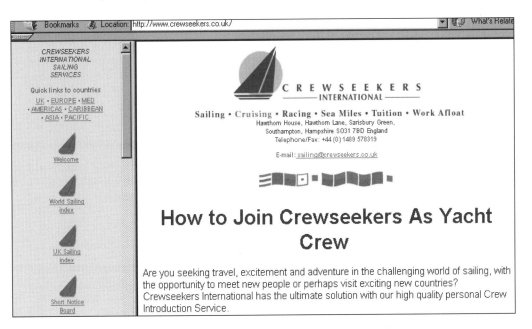

*Cruise Service Centre*
http://www.cruiseservicecenter.com
This site features current vacancies, available candidates, training programmes, and more for the cruise industry.

*Cruise Ship Jobs & Cruise Line Employment)*
http://www.freeyellow.com/members2/pme-concept/
Here you can access a worldwide directory of 350 addresses and phone numbers of the major and smaller cruise lines, a directory of 124 ship chandlers and concessionaires offering jobs on cruise ships, and a directory of 120 recruiting and crew placement agencies from around the world. There are descriptions of more than 90 different types of cruise jobs including salary. Visit the practical 'job hunter resource chapter' with full instructions on how to apply and how to prepare your résumé and cover letter. You will also information about cruise staff training institutes and schools, plus some Q&As.

# Industry-specific job sites ...............................................

*Jobs Afloat*
http://www.dorsetweb.co.uk/leisure/travelmate/publish.htm
Through this site you can access a publication on finding employment on yachts and cruise ships.

*JobXchange*
http://www.jobxchange.com
Dedicated exclusively to the global cruise and maritime industry, the International Seafarers Exchange sets up a direct connection among cruise and maritime companies, crewing agents, maritime schools, universities and prospective crew members. Interested in working in the cruise and maritime industry? You can review information on over 300 positions currently available, job descriptions, salaries, perks, life on board, regulations, policies, contracts, benefits and more. It offers opportunities with cruise lines, ferries, yachts, cargo, tanker and other maritime companies seeking to recruit and hire prospective seafarers. You can search its crew database of thousands of vacancies. The site claims to have more than 70,000 visitors from more than 100 countries each month – it's an unmissable site in its particular field.

*Ship Jobs*
http://www.shipjobs.com
Here you can find out about the big market in cruise ship jobs. Based on first hand experience, this web site offers articles, books and videos which could help your job search and career decisions.

## Public services

*British Army*
http://www.army.mod.uk/army/recruit/index2.htm
The Army has over 15,000 vacancies annually for people of all ages, abilities and educational standards. There are lots of opportunities for postings abroad.

*European Commission Representation in the UK*
http://www.cec.org.uk
This site offers good access to lots of EC information plus a vacancies section.

*International Development*
http://www.sussex.ac.uk/Units/CDU/cideve.html
Take advantage of these links developed by the Sussex University Careers Development Unit.

*RAF Careers*
http://www.raf-careers.raf.mod.uk
Here you can test your skills on a virtual mission to recover a stolen fighter plane. It is actually a hi-tech guide to the many jobs offered by Britain's airborne fighting force. If you think you fit the bill you can apply online.

Crew Homeport

Main Homeport

Member Services

Submit Resume

CrewXchange

Passport to Success

Job Descriptions

Ship Terms

Review Career Profile

Registered Companies

Testimonials

FAQ File

About the Company

*Royal Navy*
http://www.royal-navy.mod.uk
Here you can find out what's new now, what happens next, what happened when, as well as careers information.

## Science

*Science Online*
http://www.sciencemag.org
You can link into scientific job vacancies, research positions, and postings both in Europe and the USA under the Professional Network System.

*Space Careers*
http://www.spacelinks.com/SpaceCareers/
From these home pages, you can access a collection of 200-plus links to place where you can find jobs in the space and satellite industries.

## Teaching

*Appointments for Teachers*
http://www.aft.co.uk
The site mainly focuses on UK-based primary and secondary school jobs, but some overseas teaching opportunities are listed as well.

*Capstan Teachers*
http://www.capstan.co.uk/
If you are a teacher, whether UK or overseas trained, UK-based Capstan offers access to primary and secondary short and long-term posts. The site includes an introduction, guidance for students and newly qualified teachers, brief information about working in or coming from the European Union, Australia, New Zealand, United States, Canada and elsewhere.

*Educational Placement Service*
http://www.educatorjobs.com
Founded in 1973, and accredited by the National Association of Teacher Agencies, EPS says it is the largest teacher placement service in the USA. With offices all over the USA it is a private concern that recruits teachers, specialists, and administrators for public, private, parochial schools and colleges. Its job search facility is by State.

*EFL Web*
http://www.eflweb.com
This site offers articles, information, teaching jobs and resources, and practice materials for people teaching English as a foreign language (EFL), or as a second language (ESL).

*ELT Job Vacancies*
http://www.jobs.edunet.com
The TEFL Job Centre is a good contact point for English language teach-

# Industry-specific job sites ..................................................

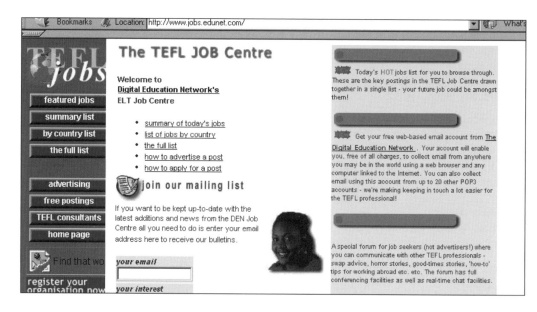

The TEFL JOB Centre

Bookmarks   Location: http://www.jobs.edunet.com/   ▼ 📬 What's

**TEFL jobs**

featured jobs
summary list
by country list
the full list

advertising
free postings
TEFL consultants
home page

Find that wo

register your
organisation now

Welcome to
**Digital Education Network's**
ELT Job Centre

* summary of today's jobs
* list of jobs by country
* the full list
* how to advertise a post
* how to apply for a post

📰 join our mailing list

If you want to be kept up-to-date with the
latest additions and news from the DEN Job
Centre all you need to do is enter your email
address here to receive our bulletins.

*your email*

*your interest*

Today's HOT jobs list for you to browse through.
These are the key postings in the TEFL Job Centre drawn
together in a single list - your future job could be amongst
them!

Get your free web-based email account from The
Digital Education Network . Your account will enable
you, free of all charges, to collect email from anywhere
you may be in the world using a web browser and any
computer linked to the Internet. You can also collect
email using this account from up to 20 other POP3
accounts - we're making keeping in touch a lot easier for
the TEFL professional!

A special forum for job seekers (not advertisers!) where
you can communicate with other TEFL professionals -
swap advice, horror stories, good-times stories, 'how-to'
tips for working abroad etc. etc. The forum has full
conferencing facilities as well as real-time chat facilities.

Fig. 52. ELT jobs from the TEFL Centre, a service of the Digital Education Network.

ing posts anywhere in the world. There is a summary of today's jobs, and a list of jobs by country. This UK centre forms part of the Digital Education Network's resources for ELT teachers, consultants and administrators internationally.

*O-Hayo Sensei (Japan)*
http://www.ohayosensei.com
*O-Hayo Sensei* is a free electronic newsletter that lists 40 to 50 teaching – and many other English language related – positions at schools and companies across Japan. Published twice a month, it presents information about salaries, skills and educational requirements, duties, benefit packages, visa requirements, housing, contracts and application procedures. It also offers readers free non-commercial ads in a lively classified section, an ongoing excerpt from a database of 2,000 schools, and a collection of Japan-related links.

*Teaching Abroad*
http://www.teaching-abroad.co.uk

*Teaching and Training Vacancies & Jobsearch*
http://www.namss.org.uk/jobs_teach.htm
This is an excellent site offering links to jobsearch guidance and resources plus several links to current vacancies in UK and US as well as links into various education and training resources. It is maintained by the National Association of Managers of Student Services.

*Teaching English as a Foreign Language and Teaching Abroad*
http://www.fedora.csu.ac.uk/Student/Cidd/booklets/teng/Bib_teng.htm
You'll find contacts and publications for teaching English abroad on this site.

*TESOL Placement Services*
http://career.tesol.edu
Visit this site for jobs and careers services.

▶ See also – *Education & Training on the Internet* by Laurel Alexander
(Internet Handbooks).

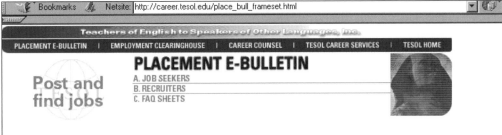

## Need an ESL/EFL job? Need it fast?

You're at the right place... TESOL's new and improved electronic job listings service, the *Placement E-Bulletin* and the members-only on-line searchable **Job Bank**. The *Placement E-Bulletin (PEB)* is sent over e-mail to TESOL members, and the Job Bank is accessible over the Web from anywhere, at any tir Members may access the Job Bank using their preferred e-mail address as their username, and their TESOL ID# as their password. Or e-mail careers@tesol.org to request your access information be sent you by e-mail.

**NEW** The most recent Placement E-Bulletin is available over the Web here for members only.

Whether you are looking for your next position or are just curious about ESL/EFL employment trends, tl *PEB* has the job listing for you! Find ESL/EFL job announcements from around the world, including Egy Japan, Yemen, Turkey, the U.S., and Mexico.

To subscribe to the *PEB*, you must be a TESOL member. E-mail careers@tesol.org and ask to sign up

# 10 Troubleshooting and emergencies

## In this chapter we will explore:

▶ *passports and visas*
▶ *travel warnings*
▶ *medical emergencies*
▶ *transportation and repatriation*
▶ *money problems*
▶ *crime*

## Passports and visas

*Travel Paperwork*
http://www.travelpaperwork.com
The site offers a useful overview of visa requirement information for 155 countries for citizens of nine nationalities, such as from North America, Australia, New Zealand, and some European countries.

*United Kingdom Passport Agency*
http://www.ukpa.gov.uk
The department deals with all aspects of application, renewal and amendment of British passports.

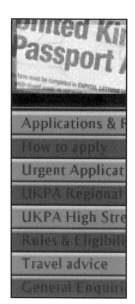

## Travel warnings

*Current Travel Warnings and Public Announcements*
http://travel.state.gov/warnings_list.html
From time to time, travel warnings are issued when the US State Department recommends that Americans avoid a certain country.

*My Travel Weather*
http://www.mytravelweather.com
Here you can look up weather conditions, weather forecasts, weather radar, UV index and other information for travel, for locations worldwide.

*Travel Information and Advisory Reports*
http://www.dfait-maeci.gc.ca/travelreport/menu_e.htm
The Canadian government issues periodic cautions relating to particular countries around the world.

*UK Foreign and Commonwealth Office: Travel Advice*
http://193.114.50.10/travel/default.asp
The travel section of the FCO website contains regularly updated information intended for British citizens on a wide range of issues concerning travelling abroad, including threats to personal safety, and a selection of consular information.

*US State Department*
http://travel.state.gov/travel_warnings.html
Travel warnings and consular information sheets can be found here.

*WEXAS*
http://www.wexas.com
WEXAS is a well-established London-based membership organisation for travellers, and offers a range of travel information, support services and contacts.

## Medical emergencies

*BUPA*
http://www.bupa.com/
The British United Provident Association is a leading UK health insurance company. In addition to providing health cover for UK residents, it is less well known that its international division covers nearly one million people in 190 countries. The site gives extensive details of the group's vast range of services, hospitals, dental cover, screening centres, care of the elderly, and recruitment opportunities.

*HospitalWeb*
http://neuro-www.mgh.harvard.edu/hospitalweb.shtml
Hosted at Harvard University, this web page contains hyperlinks to hundreds of hospital web sites on the world wide web. The links are arranged by country.

Fig. 53. HospitalWeb is a good place to locate hospitals and clinics all over the world.

MASTA
http://www.masta.org
The web site of Medical Advisory Services for Travellers Abroad offers advice on avoiding disease risks.

# Troubleshooting and emergencies ....................................

*Medical Record*
http://www.medicalrecord.com
Travellers can create and maintain vital health and contact information for free in a secure online database that can be accessed from anywhere in the world.

*Passport Health*
http://www.passporthealthusa.com
This is an example of a USA-based company which offers health advice and consultations to travellers.

*PPP Health Care*
http://www.ppphealthcare.co.uk
PPP offers medical and dental insurance and care services for individuals and companies throughout the world, and is the UK operation of the global AXA group. The site has links to: customer services, making a claim, your claim form, adding family members, complaints procedure, your questions answered, cover details, making a claim, health information, health info email, a directory of hospitals, and more.

*The Samaritans*
http://www.samaritans.org
The Samaritans is a registered charity based in the UK and Republic of Ireland that provides confidential emotional support to any person who is suicidal or despairing. An email support service is available from:

http://www.samaritans.org.hk

*Travel Doctor*
http://www.traveldoctor.com.au
This Australian company provides travel medicine and vaccination services through a network of Australian, New Zealand and SE Asian clinics. You can check out travel health reports for many destinations.

*Travel Health Online*
http://www.tripprep.com
Health information is categorised by type of illness, and by destination. There is also a list of travel medicine providers.

*Travel Health UK*
http://www.travelhealth.co.uk
The site offers practical advice on such topics as preventing accidents, stress, insurance, family holidays, mature and disabled travellers, sexual health, and animal bites.

*Travel Health Zone*
http://www.travelhealthzone.com
The site contains articles, destination-specific information, and advice from a doctor.

*Travelling Well*
http://www.travellingwell.com.au
Special reports cover topics such as travelling in Australia, IBD, asthma, Q fever, Peru, and business travel.

## Transportation and repatriation

*Passenger Rights*
http://www.passengerrights.com
The site includes a travel complaint registry, travel tips, passenger rights, and more.

*Traveler's Emergency Network*
http://www.tenweb.com
TEN is an international Florida-based organisation which provides world-wide medical assistance, 24 hour access to medical experts, emergency evacuation and repatriation home including for dependents. Membership brings access to medical facilities around the world, referrals and treatments, medical and emergency monitoring, payment for lifesaving evacuations, medical expense advances, insurance claims assistance, and other services.

*Understanding Expatriate Travel Insurance*
http://www.escapeartist.com/efam9/travel_insurance.html
This is a useful article on the Escape Artist web site which deals with emergency medical evacuation, emergency reunion, and repatriation benefit.

## Money problems

*American Express*
http://home3.americanexpress.com/uk/

*Barclaycard*
http://www.barclaycard.co.uk

*British Insurance Brokers Association*
http://www.biba.org.uk/
A contact point for insurance brokers across the UK.

*Diners Club*
http://www.citibank.com/uk/diners/new_vis/about.htm
Diners Club is part of Citibank, a company that offers US dollar credit cards to British citizens.

*Times Money: Emergency Cash*
http://www.times-money.co.uk/travel/money/money3.html
This useful article explains what to do if you want to send money to a relative living abroad, using Western Union, Moneygram, Transcheq or various other services.

# Troubleshooting and emergencies .....................................

*Mastercard*
http://www.mastercard.com

*Visa*
http://www.visa.com

*Western Union Financial Services*
http://www.westernunion.com
Find out here about Western Union emergency cash transfers, sending and receiving money, bill payments, and other services.

Fig. 54. Western Union can help you out with emergency cash transfers.

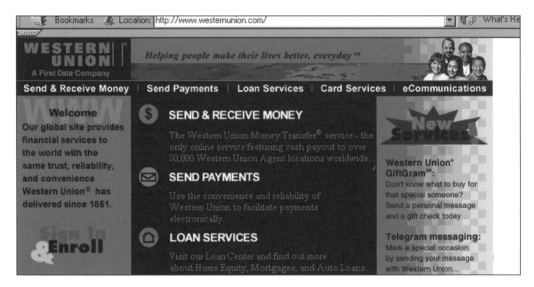

## Crime

*International Bodyguard & Security Services Association*
http://www.ibssa.com

*Interpol*
http://www.interpol.int
Interpol aims to enhance co-operation among member countries and to stimulate the exchange of information between all national and international agencies. The home page has links to news, wanted people, children and human trafficking, works of art, drugs, payment cards, forensics, vehicle crime, regional activities and terrorism.

## More Internet Handbooks to help you

*Personal Finance on the Internet*, Graham Jones.
*Medicine & Health on the Internet*, Sarah Wilkinson.
*Travel & Holidays on the Internet*, Graham Jones.

# Further reading

*Au Pair and Nanny's Guide to Working Abroad* (Vacation Work)
*Careers Guidance on the Internet*, Laurel Alexander (Internet Handbooks)
*Daily Telegraph Guide to Working Abroad*, Godfrey Golzen (Kogan Page)
*Find Temporary Work Abroad*, Nick Vandome (How To Books)
*Finding a Job on the Internet*, Brendan Murphy (Internet Handbooks, 2nd edition)
*Graduate Job Hunting on the Internet*, Laurel Alexander (Internet Handbooks)
*Teaching Abroad*, Roger Jones (How To Books)
*Where to Find It on the Internet*, Kye Valongo (Internet Handbooks, 2nd edition)
*Working from Home on the Internet*, Laurel Alexander (Internet Handbooks)
*Working in the European Communities* (CRAC)
*Working on Contract Worldwide*, Rod Briggs (How To Books)

# Glossary of internet terms

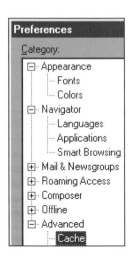

**access provider** – The company that provides you with access to the internet. See also **internet service provider**.

**ActiveX** – A Microsoft programming language that allows effects such as animations, games and other interactive features to be included a web page.

**Adobe Acrobat** – A type of software required for reading PDF files ('portable document format').

**address book** – A directory in a web browser where you can store people's email addresses.

**ADSL** – Asymmetric Digital Subscriber Line, phone line technology designed to provide a much fast internet connection speed.

**AOL** – America OnLine, the world's biggest internet service provider, with some 27 million subscribers.

**Apple Macintosh** – A type of computer that has its own proprietary operating system, as distinct from the MSDOS and Windows operating systems found on PCs (personal computers).

**applet** – An application programmed in Java that is designed to run only on a web browser.

**application** – Any program, such as a word processor or spreadsheet program, designed for use on your computer.

**ARPANET** – Advanced Research Projects Agency Network, an early form of the internet.

**ASCII** – American Standard Code for Information Interchange. It is a simple text file format that can be accessed by most word processors and text editors.

**attachment** – A file sent with an email message.

**bandwidth** – The width of the electronic highway that gives you access to the internet. The higher the bandwidth, the wider this highway, and the faster the traffic can flow.

**baud rate** – The data transmission speed in a modem, measured in kps (kilobits per second).

**BBS** – Bulletin board service. A facility to read and to post public messages on a particular web site.

**Blue Ribbon Campaign** – An internet free speech campaign. See: www.eff.org

**bookmarks** – A file of URLs of your favourite internet sites. In the Internet Explorer browser and AOL they are called Favorites.

**Boolean search** – A search in which you type in words such as AND and OR to refine your search. Such words are called 'Boolean operators'.

**bot** – Short for robot. It is used to refer to a program that will perform a task on the internet, such as carrying out a search.

**browser** – Your browser is the program that you use to access the world wide web, and manage your personal communications and privacy when online. By far the two most popular browsers are Netscape Navigator and its dominant rival Microsoft Internet Explorer.

**bug** – A weakness in a program or a computer system.

**bulletin board** – A type of computer-based news service that provides an email service and a file archive.

**cache** – A file storage area on a computer. Your web browser will normally cache (copy to your hard drive) each web page you visit.

**certificate** – A computer file that securely identifies a person or organisation on the internet.

**channel (chat)** – Place where you can chat with other internet chatters. The name of a chat channel is prefixed with a hash mark, #.

**client** – This is the term given to the program that you use to access the internet. For example your web browser is a web client, and your email program is an email client.

**configure** – To set up, or adjust the settings, of a computer or software program.

**content** – The text, articles, images, columns and sales messages of a web site.

**cookie** – A cookie is a small text code that the server of a web page asks your browser to store on your hard drive. It may be used to store password or registration details, and pass information about your site usage to the web site concerned.

**cracker** – Someone who breaks into computer systems.

**crash** – What happens when a computer program malfunctions.

**cyberspace** – Popular term for the intangible 'place' where you go to surf - the ethereal world of computers and telecommunications on the internet.

**data** – Information. Data can exist in many forms such as numbers in a spreadsheet, text in a document, or as binary numbers stored in a computer's memory.

**database** – A store of information in digital form. Many web sites make use of substantial databases to deliver maximum content at high speed to the web user.

**dial up account** – This allows you to connect your computer to your internet provider's computer remotely.

**digital** – Based on the two binary digits, 1 and 0. The operation of all computers is based on this amazingly simple concept. All forms of information are capable of being digitised - numbers, words, and even sounds and images - and then transmitted over the internet.

**directory** – On a PC, a folder containing your files.

**DNS** – Domain name server.

**domain name** – A name that identifies an IP address. It identifies to the computers on the rest of the internet where to access particular information. Each domain has a name. For someone@somewhere.co.uk, 'somewhere.co.uk' is the domain name.

**download** – To copy a file from one computer on the internet to your own computer.

**ebusiness** – The broad concept of doing business to business, and business to consumer sales, over the internet.

**ecash** – Short for electronic cash.

**ecommerce** – The various means and techniques of transacting business online.

**email** – Electronic mail, any message or file you send from your computer to another computer using your 'email client' program (such as Netscape Messenger or Microsoft Outlook).

**email address** – The unique address given to you by your ISP. It can be used by others using the internet to send email messages to you.

**emoticons** – Popular symbols used to express emotions in email, for example the well known smiley :-) which means 'I'm smiling!' Emoticons are not normally appropriate for business communications.

**encryption** – The scrambling of information to make it unreadable without a key or password.

**ezines** – The term for magazines and newsletters published on the internet.

**FAQs** – Frequently asked questions.

**Favorites** – The rather coy term for **bookmarks** used by Internet Explorer, and by America Online.

**file** – Any body of data such as a word processed document, a spreadsheet, a database file, a graphics or video file, sound file, or computer program.

**filtering software** – Software loaded into a computer to prevent access to unwelcome content on the internet.

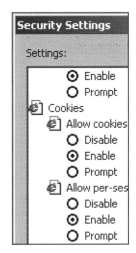

Dial-Up Networking

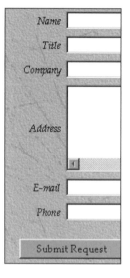

**firewall** – A firewall is special security software designed to stop the flow of certain files into and out of a computer network.

**flame** – A more or less hostile or aggressive message posted in a newsgroup or to an individual newsgroup user.

**folder** – The name for a directory on a computer. It is a place in which files are stored.

**form** – A web page that allows or requires you to enter information into fields on the page and send the information to a web site, program or individual on the web.

**forums** – Places for discussion on the internet. They include Usenet newsgroups, mailing lists, and bulletin board services.

**frames** – A web design feature in which web pages are divided into several areas or panels, each containing separate information.

**freespace** – An allocation of free web space by an internet service provider or other organisation.

**freeware** – Software programs made available without charge. Where a small charge is requested, the term is **shareware**.

**FTP** – File transfer protocol, the method the internet uses to speed files back and forth between computers.

**GIF** – Graphic interchange format. It is a widely-used compressed file format used on web pages and elsewhere to display files that contain graphic images. See also **JPEG** and **PDF**.

**hacker** – A person interested in computer programming, operating systems, the internet and computer security. In common usage, the term is often wrongly used to describe crackers.

**History list** – A record of visited web pages, stored by your browser.

**hits** – The number of times that items on a web page have been viewed.

**home page** – The index or main page of a web site.

**host** – A host is the computer where a particular file or domain is located, and from where people can retrieve it.

**HTML** – Hyper text markup language, the universal computer language used to create pages on the world wide web.

**HTTP** – Hypertext transfer protocol, the protocol used by the world wide web.

**hyperlink** – See **link**.

**hypertext** – This is a link on an HTML page that, when clicked with a mouse, results in a further HTML page or graphic being loaded into view on your browser.

**ICQ** – A form of internet chat, derived from the phrase 'I seek you'.

**internet** – A broad term that encompasses email, web pages, internet chat, newsgroups, mailing lists, bulletin boards, and video conferencing.

**internet2** – A new form of the internet being developed exclusively for educational and academic use.

**internet directory** – A special web site which consists of categorised information about other web sites. The most widely used is Yahoo! at: www.yahoo.com

**Internet Explorer** – The world's most popular browser software, a product of Microsoft.

**Internet protocol number** – The numerical code that is a domain name's real address.

**internet service providers** – Organisations which offer people ('users') access to the internet. The well-known commercial ones in the UK include AOL, CompuServe, BT Internet, Freeserve, Demon and Virgin Net. Services typically include access to the world wide web, email and newsgroups, as well as others such as news, chat, and entertainment.

**intranet** – Software that uses internet technology to allow communication between individuals, for example within a large commercial organisation. It often operates on a LAN (local area network).

**IP address** – An 'internet protocol' address. All computers linked to the internet have one. The address is somewhat like a telephone number, and consists of four sets of numbers separated by dots.

**IRC** – Internet relay chat. The chat involves typing messages which are sent and read in real time

**ISDN** – Integrated services digital network, a high-speed telephone network for internet use.

**JPEG** or **JPG** – The acronym is short for Joint Photographic Experts Group. A JPEG is a specialised file format used to display graphic files on the internet, typically colour photographs.

**kick** – To eject someone from a chat channel.

**LAN** – A local area network, a computer network usually located in one building or campus.

**link** – A hypertext phrase or image that calls up another web page when you click on it.

**LINX** – The London Internet Exchange, the facility which maintains UK internet traffic in the UK.

**listserver** – An automated email system whereby subscribers are able to receive and send email from other subscribers to the list.

**lurk** – The slang term used to describe reading a newsgroup's messages without actually taking part in that newsgroup. Despite the connotations of the word, it is a perfectly respectable activity on the internet.

**macros** – 'Macro languages' are used to automate repetitive tasks in Word processors and other applications.

**mail server** – A remote computer that enables you to send and receive emails.

**mailing list** – A forum where messages are distributed by email to the members of the forum.

**metasearch engine** – A site that sends a keyword search to many different search engines and directories so you can use many search engines from one place.

**modem** – An internal or external piece of hardware plugged into your PC. It links into a standard phone socket, thereby giving you access to the internet. The word derives from MOdulator/DEModulator.

**moderator** – A person in charge of a mailing list, newsgroup or forum.

**MPEG** or **MPG** – The file format used for video clips available on the internet. See also JPEG. See http://mpeg.org for further technical information

**MP3** – An immensely popular audio format that allows you to download and play music on your computer.

**navigate** – To click on the hyperlinks on a web site in order to move to other web pages or internet sites.

**net** – A slang term for the internet. In the same way, the world wide web is often just called the web.

**netiquette** – Popular term for the unofficial rules and language people follow to keep electronic communication in an acceptably polite form.

**Netscape** – After Microsoft's Internet Explorer, Netscape Navigator is the most popular browser software for surfing the internet.

**newsgroup** – A Usenet public discussion group. There are around 80,000 of them, arranged in hierarchies.

**newsreader** – A type of software that enables you to search, read, post and manage messages in a newsgroup. The best known are Microsoft Outlook, and Netscape Messenger.

**news server** – A remote computer (e.g. your internet service provider) that enables you to access newsgroups.

Quick Click Menu

Site Map
IRC Introduction
Newbies FAQ
IRC & Web Security

IRC Network Basics
IRC Networks
IRC Commands

mIRC Central
mIRC Installation

Getting Started

My.MP3
MP3.com Mess
Store - Free Extr

**Free Music**

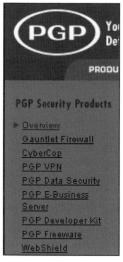

**QuickTime™**

**nick** – Nickname, an alias you can give yourself and use when entering a chat channel, rather than using your real name.

**OS** – The operating system in a computer, for example MS DOS (Microsoft Disk Operating System), or Windows 95/98.

**patch** – A small piece of software used to patch up ('fix') a hole or defect ('bug') in a software program.

**PC** – Personal computer, based on IBM technology. It is distinct from the Apple Macintosh which uses a different operating system

**PDA** – Personal data assistant, a mobile phone, palm top or any other hand-held processor, typically used to access the internet.

**PDF** – Portable document format, a handy type of file produced using Adobe Acrobat software. It has universal applications for text and graphics.

**PGP** – Pretty Good Privacy, a proprietary and highly secure method of encoding a message before transmitting it over the internet.

**plug-in** – A type of (usually free and downloadable) software required to add some form of functionality to web page viewing, such as Macromedia Shockwave.

**PoP** – Point of presence. This refers to the dial-up phone numbers available from your ISP.

**portal site** – Portal means gateway. It is a web site designed to serve as a general jumping off point into the internet or to some particular part of it.

**privacy** – To explore internet privacy issues worldwide visit the Electronic Frontier Foundation at www.eff.org, and for the UK, www.netfreedom.org

**protocol** – Technical term for the method by which computers communicate.

**proxy** – An intermediate computer or server, used for reasons of security.

**Quicktime** – A popular free software program from Apple Computers. It is designed to play sounds and images including video clips and animations on both Apple Macs and personal computers.

**radio button** – A button that, when clicked, looks like this: ⊙

**refresh, reload** – The refresh or reload button on your browser toolbar tells the web page you are looking at to reload.

**register** – You may have to give your name, personal details and financial information to some sites before you can continue to use the pages.

**RIP** – The Regulation of Investigatory Powers Act, a UK law passed in 2000 which enables the police to carry out surveillance of internet users, using so-called 'black boxes' installed at internet service providers.

**router** – A machine that directs internet data (network packets) from one internet location to another.

**script** – A script is a set of commands written into the HTML tags of a web page.

**scroll, scroll bar** – To scroll means to move part of a page or document into view or out of view on the screen. Scrolling is done by using a scroll bar activated by the mouse pointer. Grey scroll bars automatically appear on the right and/or lower edge of the screen if the page contents are too big to fit into view.

**search engine** – A search engine is a web site you can use for finding something on the internet. The technology variously involves the use of 'bots' (search robots), spiders or crawlers. Popular search engines have developed into big web sites and information centres in their own right. Among the best known are AltaVista, Excite, Google, Infoseek , Lycos, Metasearch and Webcrawler.

**secure sockets layer (SSL)** – A standard piece of technology which ensures secure financial transactions and data flow over the internet.

**server** – Any computer on a network that provides access and serves information to other computers.

**shareware** – Software that you can try before you buy. Usually there is some kind of limitation such as an expiry date.

**Shockwave** – A popular piece of software, or plug-in, produced by Macromedia, which enables you to view animations and other special effects on web sites.

**signature file** – This is a little text file in which you can place your address details, for adding to email and newsgroup messages.

**smiley** – A form of **emoticon**.

**snail mail** – The popular term for the standard postal service involving post-persons, vans, trains, planes, sacks and sorting offices.

**sniffer** – A program on a computer system (usually an ISP's system) designed to collect information about internet use.

**spam** – Electronic junk mail.

**SSL** – Secure socket layer, a key part of internet security technology.

**subscribe** – The term for accessing a newsgroup or internet mailing list in order to read and post messages.

**surfing** – Slang term for browsing the internet, especially following trails of links on pages across the world wide web.

**TCP/IP** – Transmission control protocol/internet protocol, the essential technology of the internet.

**telnet** – Software that allows you to connect via the internet to a remote computer and work as if you were a terminal linked to that system.

**thread** – An ongoing topic in a Usenet newsgroup or mailing list discussion. The term refers to the original message on a particular topic, and all the replies and other messages which spin off from it.

**thumbnail** – A small version of a graphic file which, when clicked, displays a larger version.

**top level domain** – The last piece of code in a domain name, such as .com or .uk

**traffic** – The amount of data flowing across the internet, to a particular web site, newsgroup or chat room, or as emails.

**trojan horse** – A program that seems to perform a useful task but is really a malevolent program designed to cause damage to a computer system.

**UNIX** – A computer operating system that has been in use for many years, mostly by larger systems.

**uploading** – The act of copying files from your PC to a server or other PC on the internet, for example when you are publishing your own web pages.

**URL** – Uniform resource locator, the address of each internet page. For instance the URL of Internet Handbooks is http://www.internet-handbooks.co.uk

**Usenet** – The collection of some 80,000 public newsgroups that make up a substantial part of the internet.

**virtual reality** – The presentation of a lifelike scenario in electronic form. It can be used for gaming, business or educational purposes.

**virus** – A computer program maliciously designed to cause havoc to people's computer files.

**web authoring** – Creating HTML pages to upload onto the internet.

**web** – Short for the world wide web. See **WWW** below.

**WAP** – Wireless application protocol, new technology that enables mobile phones to access the internet.

**webmaster** – Any person who manages a web site.

**web rings** – A network of interlinked web sites that share a common interest.

**web site** – A set of web pages, owned or managed by the same person or organisation, and which are interconnected by hyperlinks.

**Windows** – The operating system for personal computers developed by Bill Gates and the Microsoft Corporation. Windows 3.1 was followed by Windows 95, further enhanced by Windows 98. Windows 2000 is the latest.

**wizard** – A feature of many software programs that guides you through its main stages.

**WWW** – The world wide web. Since it began in 1994 this has become the most

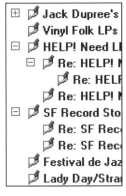

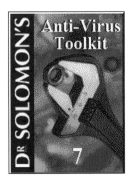

# Glossary of internet terms ..........................................

popular part of the internet. The web is now made up of more than a billion web pages of every imaginable description, typically linking to other pages.

**WYSIWYG** – 'What you see is what you get.' If you see it on the screen, then it should look just the same when you print it out.

**Yahoo!** – Probably the world's most popular internet directory and search engine.

# Index

# Index....................................................